MY BEST DAY
THE DAY AFTER YESTERDAY

Copyright © 2024 by Stephen Williford

Printed and Produced in the United States of America

All rights reserved. No part of this book may be reproduced or utilized in any form or by any means, electronic or mechanical, including photocopying, recording, or by any information storage and retrieval system, without permission in writing from the Publisher, except by a reviewer who wishes to quote brief passages in connection with a review written for inclusion in a magazine, newspaper, broadcast, or webpage.

Inquiries should be addressed to:
Permissions Dept., Radian Partners

For media and other inquiries contact:
Larry J. Tolbert, Publisher
larry.tolbert@radianpartners.net
6055 Primacy Parkway, Suite 160
Memphis, TN 38119
Office 901.202.3909
Fax 901.202.3975

Interior and exterior design by Louise Koonce, LuraeDesigns
Special thanks to Don DeWeese for digitizing photographs

There have been five very special people in my life and I'd like to dedicate this book to them.

To Jeannie, Sunny, Cindy, Major, and Priscilla.

I love you,
Haywood

> Life doesn't end for us just because we retire or get a little older. I'm of the opinion that every day should be our best day. Each day is not about our limitations but what we make of that day regardless of any limits we might have. It's the beauty we find in each day.

Haywood Smith

PREFACE

It has been my pleasure to have known Haywood Smith since we were together in Vietnam.

My first tour in Vietnam was as a platoon leader and then as commanding officer of K Company 3rd Battalion 5th Marines (K/3/5). My second tour was as an aerial observer/tactical air controller assigned to Marine Observation Squadron 2 (VMO-2) at Marble Mountain expeditionary airfield near Da Nang.

Colonel Haywood Smith commanded the Marine Air Group (MAG 16) which included helicopters and OV10A Broncos flown by VMO-2. I can assure you that going into a "hot LZ" in Vietnam in an assault helicopter like the CH46 was a "tough way to make a living." The Group CO would not be expected to fly the number of missions Col. Smith did. The record shows that he flew over 200 combat sorties.

Since those days, Haywood and I have formed a friendship that I value very much. We've traveled across the country for all types of events, and hunted together, and shared many stories and memories. At various times, he's served as my confidant, and source of good yarns, and organizer of pleasant events with other great friends.

Even in his nineties, Haywood plays a skillful game of golf or poker, your choice…but don't bet! He has the rare ability to make others feel welcome and valued.

He is one of my favorite people whom I admire greatly for his remarkable and outstanding service to our country.

Frederick W. Smith
Founder and Executive Chairman, FedEx

INTRODUCTION FROM THE AUTHOR

I have written a lot of books for a lot of people. But I have never come across a story like that of Haywood Smith. Here are a few reasons that I feel that way:

- Seated between actress Janet Leigh and Werner von Braun at a formal White House State Dinner, Haywood thought, "This is pretty good duty. On one side of me is the best-looking woman in the world, and on the other is arguably the smartest man on the planet. I wonder what they're thinking about me?"

- As Military Aide to U.S. President Lyndon Johnson, Haywood accompanied the President, carrying the briefcase, aka the "football," containing the nuclear launch codes, and serving as an Air Force One co-pilot.

- Fearless and fun-loving, he once "borrowed" the President's jet to sneak down to St. Louis for a World Series game at the invitation of his good friend, Stan Musial. No one ever found out... until now.

- While serving as commander of the Marble Mountain Marine Base in Vietnam, Colonel Smith flew over two hundred missions, many more than required, receiving enemy fire.

- We were sitting on Haywood's back patio overlooking the golf course, watching the sunset, when he tells me, "People should learn to laugh. It's kept me going in the strangest places."

Stephen Williford

Me with my little sister.

We are very fortunate to have so many photographs, many of them more than fifty years old. We acknowledge that, while some are low resolution and some not in perfect focus, they provide a dramatic account of Haywood Smith's best days.

TABLE OF CONTENTS

CHAPTER ONE **13**
   Beginnings

CHAPTER TWO **25**
   The Few, The Proud, The Marines

CHAPTER THREE **41**
   Serving at the Pleasure of the President

CHAPTER FOUR **107**
   Back to the Corps

CHAPTER FIVE **155**
   Life After 'Nam

CHAPTER SIX **173**
   From Those Who Know Him Best

CHAPTER SEVEN **207**
   From Haywood

EPILOGUE **216**
   From the Author

INDEX **219**

This is me with my grandmother, aunt and sister.

They nicknamed me Sonny.

CHAPTER ONE
BEGINNINGS

WHERE IT ALL BEGAN

Haywood Smith was born in a small South Memphis house and raised primarily by his grandparents, Muddy and Pops. In fact, he spent most of his early life with them in their two-bedroom brick house, a few blocks away on Rosewood. Muddy and Pops slept in one bedroom and his mother and sister shared the other one, while Haywood slept in the dining room.

As a student at Lauderdale Elementary, Haywood was more interested in playing marbles than schoolwork, which didn't please Muddy at all. According to Haywood, they drew the circle, and the game was on. They played for keeps. He lost his share of marbles, but he won more. However, it seems that winning didn't keep him from being in trouble with Muddy.

"I wasn't a good student in those days, but Miss Minnie saved me. She really took to me and thought I was the cat's meow. I never would have finished first or second grade if it wasn't for her!"

EARLY JOBS

Haywood started working at an early age. At fifteen, he worked with two other boys on the barges alongside the river. They worked in the shop handing out the tools for the workers.

I loved baseball from as early as I could throw a ball.

Life was good for me as I grew up with Muddy and Pops. I didn't realize how little we had, but they provided everything I needed.

The Pine Hill Golf Course was only two blocks away from Muddy and Pop's house, so on Saturdays and Sundays, he caddied there beginning when he was 13. Not only did he get paid a dollar for eighteen holes, but he also got interested in golf. He acquired a set of women's clubs and started playing.

"I would sneak over and play a few holes. I would get balls by hiding in a gully where I knew a lot of players would hit out of bounds. I would watch the ball go in and slip over and pick it up."

He enjoys the game and still plays to this day. There are many golf tournament trophies scattered throughout his home.

His caddy career was followed by being a lifeguard, something he did for many years. From this, he became a good three-meter springboard diver. He and his friends traveled to exotic destinations like Florida, to put on diving shows for the payment of room and board. That was a good deal for Haywood and his diving crew. It was in the late 40's and they loved Florida. They didn't have any money, but it didn't cost them much. Sometimes they took a car, but most of the time, they hitchhiked. Many drivers would pick them up, no questions asked. "It is not like that these days," he recalled. "Only one or two cars would pass before somebody would pick you up."

When a kind driver stopped, he would ask, "Where you going, son?"

"I would tell them where and they would say, they weren't going that far but they would take me part of the way."

One time, Haywood hitchhiked while the others were in a car with Bags Brenner, who played football for Ole Miss. "I beat them down to Florida. They couldn't believe it."

Haywood and his friends would also "hop" trucks. When the trucks went up the hill slowly, they would jump on and just ride to wherever it went. The driver wouldn't know it. One time Haywood and his friend hopped on a gasoline tanker truck. They climbed up the ladder on the side to take a seat on the top of the tanker. They were riding that truck from Memphis to Sardis Lake where there was a big dam to dive from. "It was a very good spot, beautiful."

He asked his friend, "How are we going to get off of this truck?"

Man, I was a good looking kid. I had no clue what I was going to do. As a matter of fact, if you had told me what my future held, I wouldn't have believed you.

The truck was going fast. As they held on tight, his friend said, "I don't know."

So, when they got close to where they wanted to get off and started beating on the side of the truck.

"He pulled that truck over and we got down and ran. But we got where we were going."

AN EARLY LESSON IN CHURCH BEHAVIOR

"When I was about 12, Muddy always made sure that I was at Bellevue Baptist Church in downtown Memphis. Bellevue was a large church with several thousand members at that time. She would give me a quarter to put in the collection plate. I would often get the quarter changed into five nickels. I would put 20 cents in the plate, which left me a nickel to play some pinball.

"On one particular Sunday, I was sitting with my friends in the balcony. We were not paying attention to Dr. Robert Greene Lee's sermon. As a matter of fact, we were talking and giggling.

"Toward the conclusion of his talk, we decided to leave a little early. So we stood up and headed for the stairs. Unfortunately, Dr. Lee noticed us. He stopped his sermon and said, "You boys in the balcony." Everyone turned around and looked at us. "I want you to sit down and wait until our service is over before you leave. And next week, I expect better behavior from each of you."

"Unfortunately, Muddy was sitting in that audience that turned to see who Dr. Lee was addressing. Later that day, she told me how disappointed she was in me. And the look in her eyes was the worst thing she could have done. She told me that I was not just disrespectful to Dr. Lee, but to the Lord.

"From that day, you better believe that I have been respectful of worship services and respectful to the Lord.

"And . . . I put the full quarter in the collection plate."

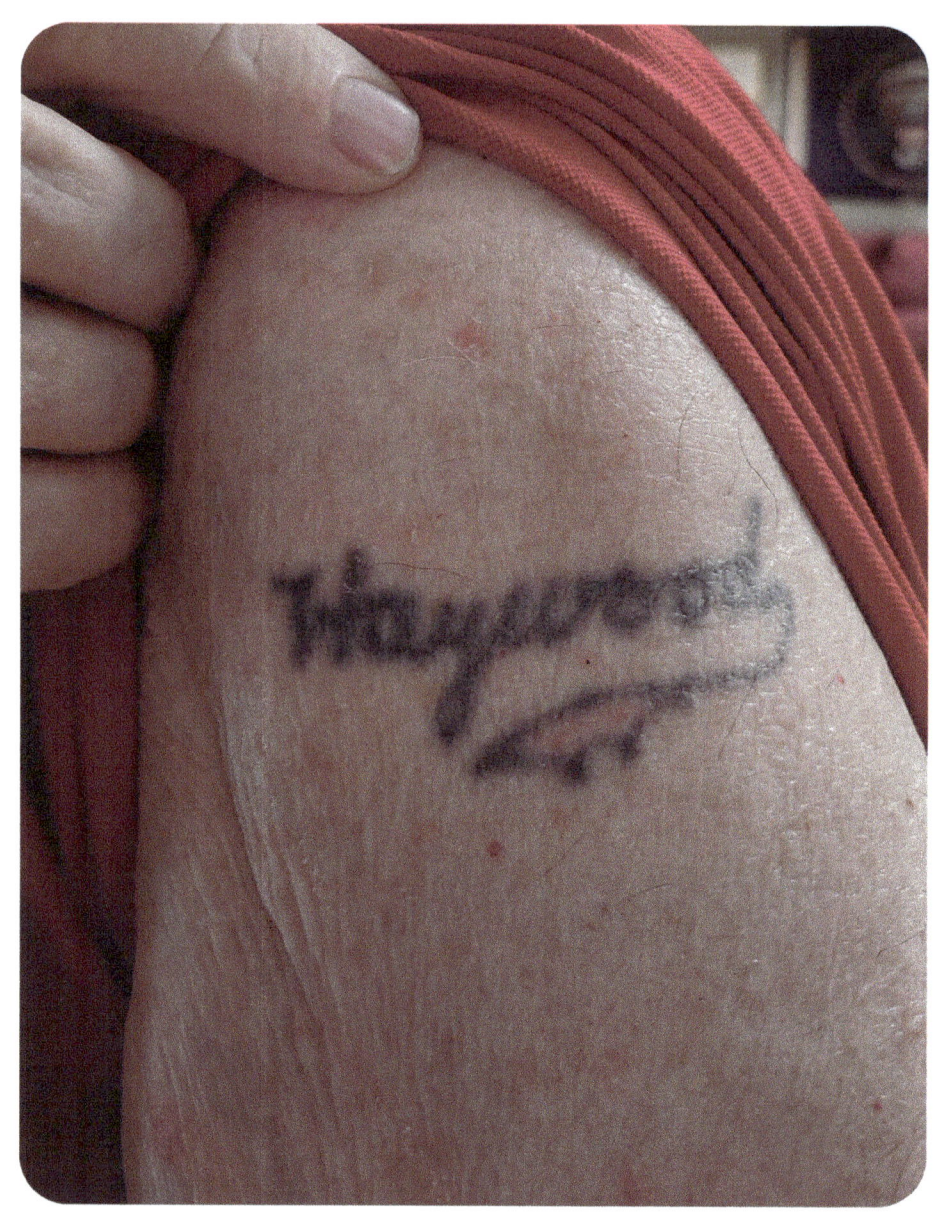

This tattoo got me in hot water with Muddy, but has stuck with me all these years.

18 MY BEST DAY

THE TATTOO LADY

When Haywood was 16, he and a group of boys decided to take another trip to Florida. Somehow, a couple of them had cars, and they decided they were going to go to Key West, 1,200 miles away.

They had "big fun." on the way, sleeping in the car and finding places to swim. Once they got to Key West, they walked all over the place, just scouting things out. Eventually, they came across a tattoo parlor. Inside was the most beautiful woman they had ever seen. All were convinced that she was meant to fall in love with one of them.

But the question was, how would they get her attention? The answer? Obviously, they all needed to get a tattoo! That would be when she would choose one of the promising 16-year-olds to live the rest of her life with. Even at $2.75 per tattoo, they were willing to pay the price for destiny to take its course.

They decided to get tattoos on their arms up by their shoulders. When they walked in, the beautiful Tattoo Lady didn't look too thrilled. She told them to get in line. She went down the line and wrote their names on a sheet of paper.

One of the boys, Ed, went to use the bathroom. When he came back, he took a different place in line. Well, the Tattoo Lady was continuing to put each person's name on his arm. About that time, one of the guys, Buddy, yelled, "Hey, I'm not Ed!" She had scripted Ed's name on the wrong person!

Sadly, the beautiful Tattoo Lady didn't fall in love with any of them. They left Florida, all still single but tattooed, and returned home.

When he got back home, Muddy saw *Haywood* on his arm and ordered, "You go wash that ink off right now!" He said, "Yes ma'am," and left the room to put on a shirt.

Five months later, she saw it again and said, "I told you. Get that ink off." This time, she got a washcloth and tried to wash it off. After scrubbing with no effect, she started screaming so much, he thought she was going to have a heart attack. 75 years later, the Colonel can still be identified by the cursive *Haywood* on his bicep.

During High School, I joined the boxing team. It turns out that I won the Golden Gloves trophy for the city of Memphis.

This is my senior class picture from Tech High School, class of 1948.

HIGH SCHOOL SHENANIGANS

The fear of Muddy and the switches that came from her backyard kept Haywood out of much trouble in high school. He graduated from Bellevue Junior High and many of his friends were going to Tech High School. Muddy agreed and allowed him to take the streetcar daily to go to Tech.

One time he played a joke on Miss Campbell, the second-floor history teacher. He and his good friend Jim were both failing history class. So, they decided they had to do something, and made a plan.

This is how the plan unfolded:

They both wore grey pants and a red shirt. Haywood was in the classroom, and said, "Miss Campbell, if you don't pass Jim and me, I'm going to jump out that window."

"Oh no, you're not!" she said. "But you will learn to respect my class!"

Haywood just shook his head and said, "I warned you." He climbed out of the open window onto the ledge outside.

All the students yelled, "Miss Campbell, he jumped!" She ran to the window and looked down and there Jim was laying on the ground below in those grey pants and red shirt just like Haywood! As Haywood remembers, Miss Campbell had to take a few days off.

"Oh boy. Miss Campbell just about died, but we passed history! It was really self-preservation. I don't think she could take another year of Jim and me."

THE CASE OF THE WATERMELON HEIST

Haywood was also known to steal a watermelon or two. The trucks would come into Memphis from surrounding counties, and there was a big hill they would have to climb coming into town. If it stopped at a red light, it had a hard time getting up the hill. So, he and his buddies would wait near the red light and one of them would drive his Chevrolet up close to the truck. Haywood got on the hood and when they got beside the truck, he jumped on and began handing watermelons back to the moving car. One day, the truck pulled over into a gas

I spent the summers as a lifeguard along with some of my buddies from college at Maywood Swimming Pool.
I'm the handsome one on the right.

station parking lot and there was Haywood, still in the back.

The police came and the driver said, "These boys have been stealing watermelons from me and I am tired of it!"

Haywood was taken to juvenile court and Muddy was notified. When she walked into the courtroom, she saw the watermelon positioned on the judge's bench. He explained to Muddy that they caught Haywood stealing watermelons. He looked at her and said, "I am thinking I'd like to give him a second chance if you think he isn't going to steal any more watermelons."

She said that this was the last one he would ever steal, and the judge was convinced. On the way out, Haywood asked Muddy what she thought the judge was going do with that watermelon. "She didn't think that was very funny!"

> **"My boyhood was a great season in my life. I made so many great memories with great friends. At the time, I had no idea what was in my future. And even if you had told me, I would have said you were crazy. Boy was I in for a wild ride!"**

Muddy was proud that I made the decision to join the Marines.

CHAPTER TWO
THE FEW, THE PROUD, THE MARINES

THE RESERVES AND BASEBALL

Growing up, Haywood distinctly recalled being told by his dad, "Don't you dare join the Army or Air Force!"

For once in his life, he did what he was told. When he was still in high school, he drove to Millington, Tennessee and enlisted in the Marine Corps Reserves. Maneuvers in the summer provided a paycheck. When he graduated from high school, he went straight to boot camp at Parris Island, a barrier Sea Island in Beaufort County, SC. It is home to one of the two regional Recruit Training Depots used by the United States Marine Corps.

Afterwards, he came back and went to college at the University of Memphis, then known as "Memphis State," where he received a scholarship to play baseball.

His dad was a very good baseball player. "He was a pitcher. I was a good player, too, and really thought that I could be a pro." He and his friends had played on league teams each summer when they were young. "Usually, men took time off from their jobs to coach us. So, I learned a lot from them. They and Muddy helped me stay out of trouble."

He played baseball for the University of Memphis in the Spring, and in the summertime, he played for a semi-pro team, sponsored by Coca-Cola, that played all over the Mid - South. He was paid $25 a game.

I quickly found myself training to be a fighter pilot.

This was in the training command just before I received my wings.

CAREER CHANGE FROM A CURVEBALL

"I already decided that this was going to be my chosen career. I was a solid second baseman; could play any of the positions on the infield; and I was a pretty good hitter.

So, there we were, and this guy steps on to the mound to pitch for Birmingham. They were in the Double A's, and he was warming up. My coach said that he was pretty good as a Double A pitcher. I stepped up to the plate to bat and the pitcher threw the ball. It looked like it fell off a table when it came across the plate. He struck me out.

I went back to the dugout and asked the Coach, 'Rut, this guy's pretty good. You mean there's better pitchers than him in the pros?'

Coach Rut answered, 'Awe, he ain't gonna make it in the pros.'

I said, 'I'm not either'

So, I decided to go into the Marine Corps as a Lieutenant."

> **"I had no more encouraging supporter than Col. Smith. He came to my ballgames and kept in touch by phone all through the year. I'm just a big fan of his."**
>
> *Tim McCarver, professional baseball player*

Why this beauty queen agreed to marry me, I'll never know, but I sure am glad she did.

WHY A BEAUTY QUEEN BURNED HER SWIMMING SUITS

"Jeannie was Miss Everything! She was a beauty queen and a cheerleader at Memphis State. She hated to get out in front of everyone, but she won all the contests. She was beautiful, popular, and had a pretty figure, but she was modest."

When Haywood finished college, the USMC sent him to Officer Candidate School. He planned to be in the Marines for two years. Then one day, he heard, "Fall out!" They were at Parris Island, preparing to go on a 20-mile hike. While they were standing there, a Sergeant said if anybody was interested in flight training, they needed to fall out and head to that office. Haywood didn't want to go on that twenty miler, so he fell out along with five others.

They were told to report to the center for testing. Several weeks later, while they were in formation, the Sergeant called for Smith and Taylor to fall out. They were informed that they had passed the flight test and were to report to be interviewed. Pilots served six-year terms. Taylor, the other candidate, wanted to do just that, but Lieutenant Smith still wasn't so sure he wanted to make the Marines a career. They went in for the interviews and Haywood found himself standing in front of two majors. "I had never even seen a major!"

They asked him, "Lieutenant Smith, why do you want to be a Marine Corps pilot?"

He thought about that and said, "Well, my girlfriend is a stewardess for American Airlines and I want to be a pilot so I can fly around and go see her when I want to."

They began laughing and said, "You'll do son, you'll do!"

Then it was time for him to go on a flight. "I loved it! I was hooked!"

The pilot asked him if he wanted to fly the plane a little and, just like that, Haywood had the controls. "I was having so much fun sending that plane up and down and around. "They told me to calm down. It took my breath away!"

Haywood went through flight training, then advanced training before he got his wings. "Muddy and Pops were so proud."

❝ I first met Haywood on a USO tour. I then did a show for his base in New Orleans. We found time to get together throughout the years. He made my work meaningful. **❞**

Bob Hope, entertainer, actor

As soon as he received the wings, he gave Jeannie a call. She was in Tulsa, waiting for a flight to go out. "I asked her, right then on the phone if she wanted to get married."

She said, "Well yes, I do."

So, he told her, "Well, next week I will be in Tulsa. Get everything ready and we'll get married."

The families found out and they traveled to Tulsa for the wedding! The newlyweds went to Laguna Beach after the wedding for an oceanside honeymoon.

They were staying at a hotel on that pretty beach, so Haywood said, "We need to go down there for a swim!"

Jeannie answered, "I don't have a swimsuit!"

"What do you mean you don't have a swimsuit?"

She told him that when she graduated from college and was no longer in beauty pageants, she burned all of them.

"That is how much she disliked those contests," Haywood remembered.

They were stationed near the base, only 30 minutes from the airfield. So in the afternoons, Haywood would *buzz* the house before he landed. That way, Jeannie would know he was going to be home soon.

HOW HAYWOOD BECAME GOOD FRIENDS WITH BOB HOPE

Jack Jennings recalled this story:

"When we were captains, Haywood and I had some time off and we ended up in San Juan, Jack Jennings recalled. We decided that we would go to the old San Juan Hotel for a drink and to listen to a very good band downstairs. The place was jammed. Finally, the manager came to speak to us. He saw we were in uniform and asked if we'd like a table."

"That surprised us because every table was already full. When we said that

While I was away on missions, with Muddy and Pops close by, Jeannie raised our kids and managed our home like a true Marine wife.

" If I had a nickel for every time I thought of you, I'd buy me some gum. "

we'd like to sit down, he motioned for a couple of guys to set up a table down front. So, we were enjoying the show, when, all of a sudden, they set up a table that butted up against ours. Here came four people who sat down, right next to us."

"I said to Haywood, 'Do you know who is sitting next to you?'"

"He didn't recognize him. So, when I told him it was Bob Hope, Haywood immediately turned to Bob and said, 'Well, good evening, Mr. Hope. I'm Captain Haywood Smith and this is Captain Jack Jennings.'"

"Of course, Hope was a great supporter of the military and began asking questions about where we were stationed, what we were doing, what we flew, how things were going for us and so forth."

"He discovered we were Marine pilots and asked if we knew a particular Marine General. Obviously, we had no direct contact with any General."

"Haywood simply said, 'We don't know him but we know *of* him.'"

"Haywood was in all his glory, talking to Bob Hope, and Mr. Hope really liked Haywood and couldn't quit talking to him."

"Before long, their party left. We stayed there for a bit longer and asked for our bill. That's when the manager came back and explained that Mr. Hope had taken care of it."

"I was impressed by two things about Haywood. First, his ability to captivate a celebrity when 30 seconds before he didn't even recognize him. Second is the generosity of a person who happened to be a celebrity that paid for our tab. That meant a great deal."

Haywood added this to Jack's story:

"It's a lesson I have never forgotten. There we were, two Marines, far away from home. And someone was kind enough to pay for our drinks. He cared about us. He validated us. I still remember that act 60 years later. That's why I try to pass it on to military men and women today. I encourage you to do it, too. How? If you see them in uniform at the airport, pay for their meal, upgrade their ticket, or just shake their hand and give them a smile and a word of thanks. We

That looks like me taking off of the carrier Enterprise during the Cuban Missile Crisis.

Here we are preparing for a mission in the A-4s from Key West FL.

live in a very selfish society. Acts like that stand out like a beacon and are few and far between."

PILOT HUMOR

They were going on a long flight, over the ocean, with three *plug-ins*. Just before taking off, Haywood went to fellow pilot Earl Lovell's jet, and found the hose where pilots urinate during their flight. He put some gum in there and stopped it up. So, in a little while he heard him yelling over the radio. His piddle-pack seemed to be overflowing. "I laughed so hard I couldn't breathe," Haywood said.

Another time when the squadron was coming back from deployment, they landed and stopped at the PX at Guantanamo Bay. Lovell saw that Smith was buying some cards for Jeannie and the kids and asked, "Why are you buying those cards? We're going to be home in three days."

Lovell continued to make fun of him in front of the other pilots. Haywood waited for him to leave, then bought another card and addressed it to Lovell's wife, even tracing his signature, from the logbook. Haywood sent the card, then, sort of forgot about it.

They had been gone for two months on deployment. So, after landing, the wives and the kids were all out there to welcome them back. Jeannie and the kids came up and gave Haywood a big hug. The other pilot's wife went up to him. She had a big purse that hung from a shoulder strap. Lovell held out his arms and she hit him in the face with the purse. It almost knocked him down.

Lovell came to work the next day and told Haywood, "I'm going to kill whoever sent her that card."

Haywood looked at him and asked, "What card?"

He said, "You've got to help me find out who it was, Haywood."

He thought about it for a minute and then remembered he was the one that had sent it. But he still acted innocent and asked, "What did it say?"

Lovell said, "If I had a nickel for every time I thought of you, I'd buy me some gum."

Our ground crew was so good, we took it for granted that everything was squared away before we got in the air.

He was mad and so was she. The Colonel thought maybe that wasn't such a good joke, after all. But the pilot never found out.

Until maybe now.

WHILE ON THE ENTERPRISE

The Colonel had flown jets from Key West, Florida during the Cuban Missile Crisis.

"Everybody asked me if it was hard to land a jet on a carrier. My answer was 'No, it wasn't hard.' Looking back I guess it was. But we practiced over and over until we knew what to do. We landed on a model runway, set up in the desert. After that, we had the confidence, even though the model never moved like a ship on the high seas! Truly, though, it took something more. It required that the pilots had the attitude that regardless of the conditions, we were going to hit that wire."

Haywood learned that the best pilots were not always the ones that looked like they came out of a Marine poster. "Some of the Corps' best pilots didn't look much like pilots, but they had confidence; they had skill; and they had attitude. They weren't afraid, they were ready."

THE 20 FRIDGE SALUTE TO THE USMC

As a Captain during the Cuban Missile Crisis, Smith's squadron was stationed on the Enterprise just off the South Florida coast. He had not been there long when Colonel Conger told him, "We've got so many people on base that we don't have enough places to sleep."

The Marines had tents on the Key West Coast. "While the Navy had all kinds of buildings and infrastructure, the Marines didn't have anything."

Colonel Conger called Captain Smith in and said, "I can't get any supplies for these men. I've made a lot of phone calls, but I can't get anybody to send us what we need!"

Smith asked him what he needed.

We always flew in tight formation on our missions.
I was piloting the A-4 marked #3.

"If we could just get about 20 refrigerators, that would really help." He said, "Can you think of anything we can do?"

"I'll think of something," Haywood replied. "Does it matter how I get them?"

"No."

Haywood secured ten officers and two trucks, which they drove over to Navy Housing. Not in uniform, they knocked on several doors and said, "We're supposed to remove your refrigerator so you can get a new one tomorrow."

"Oh good. Come on in."

They came back with 20 refrigerators and gave them to their enlisted Marines.

A couple of days later, the Colonel called Haywood and said, "Do you know the storm that you've kicked up?"

"Yes sir," he answered.

"The whole Navy is looking for whoever took about 20 refrigerators. Whoever it was did not have on a uniform."

And then they both proudly and simultaneously said, "Semper Fi!"

> **While the Navy had all kinds of buildings and infrastructure, the Marines didn't have anything.**

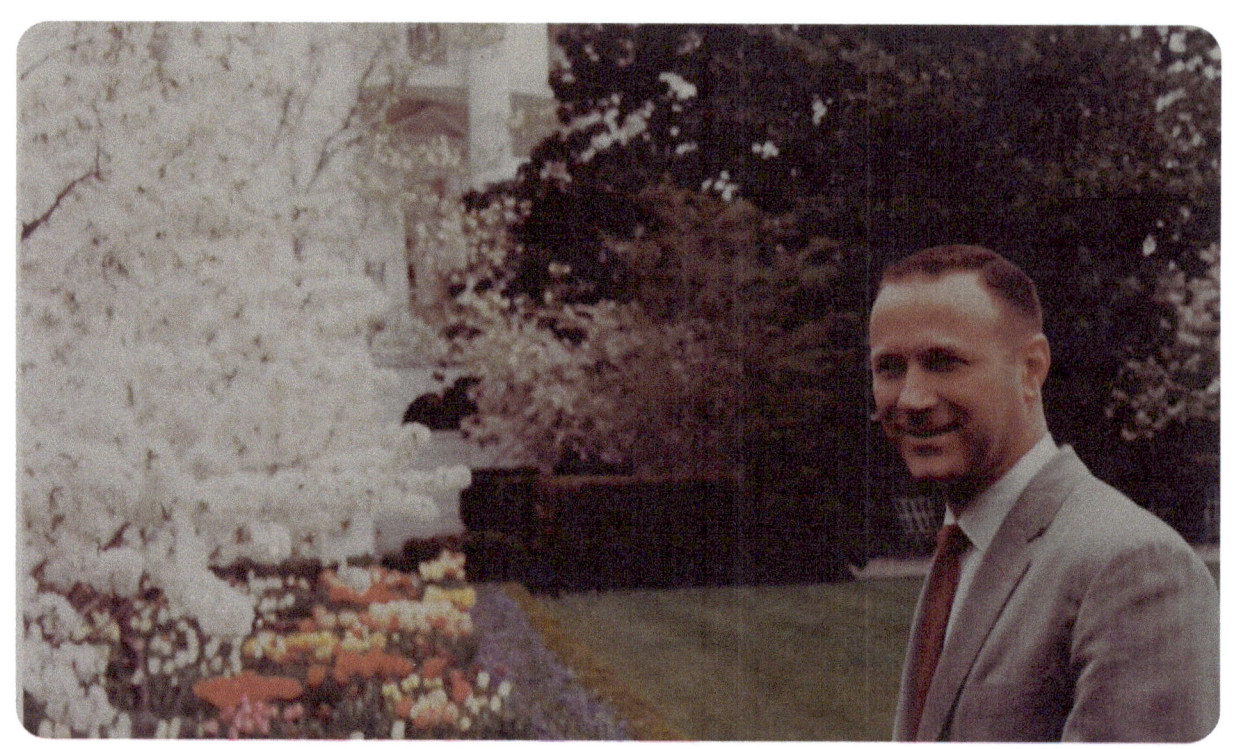

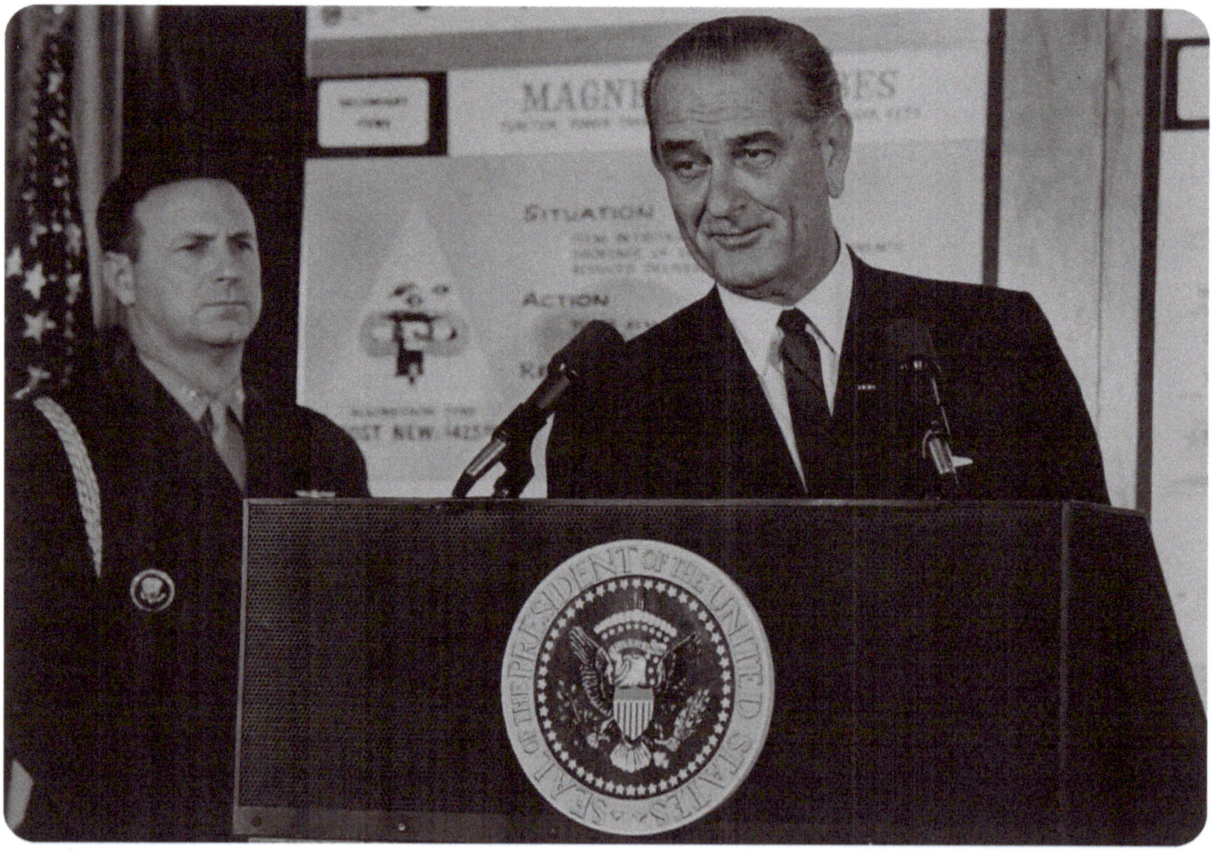
SITUATION
ACTION
SEAL OF THE PRESIDENT OF THE UNITED STATES

CHAPTER THREE
SERVING AT THE PLEASURE OF THE PRESIDENT

Author's Note - The following are stories about Haywood's time with and service to President Lyndon B. Johnson. This is the first time they have been revealed. Many of his experiences happened at President Johnson's Ranch in central Texas. Major Haywood Smith had the deepest respect and admiration for President Johnson. He also saw a great deal of humor when no one else did at the time.

MR. SMITH GOES TO WASHINGTON

Haywood had been the Operations Officer on a carrier located in the Panama Canal when he received orders to report to Washington for a job interview. He didn't want to go, but he followed orders. He was interviewed by several high-ranking officers, such as Paul Nitze, the Secretary of the Navy, and finally by Robert McNamara, the Secretary of Defense. He knew others were being interviewed for the position. One was from the Naval Academy. One was from Dartmouth. Haywood knew he was from Memphis State. He also knew there was no way he would be selected. But, to his surprise, he was selected to serve at the White House and immediately began working directly for President Johnson. He reported for duty, with no idea of what lay ahead of him.

As you can see from my position behind the President, I accompanied him to all official ceremonies.

Standing in front of the White House with the Military Aides to the President.

HOW HAYWOOD BECAME THE ARMED FORCES AIDE

President Kennedy had an Army General, a Navy Admiral, and Air Force General. They took care of all military operations. It was a huge responsibility. President Johnson wanted to simplify that by having one person in charge.

Haywood was the Marine aide. He oversaw Camp David because it was guarded by Marines. The Navy commanded the two boats there. The Air Force oversaw Air Force One. The Army was in charge of land transportation. To minimize his number of direct reports and because he wanted a Marine, President Johnson created an Armed Forces Aide role, and appointed Army General, Ted Clifton to the position, with the White House military staff all reporting to him instead of to the President. Then he would share whatever he wanted to with the President. Haywood's title was Assistant to the Armed Forces Aide to the President.

In addition to that role, Haywood helped Jim Cross with the flying of Air Force One. They were also responsible for everything on the Ranch, down to the cow pies that occasionally got left on the runway.

WHY WAS HAYWOOD SMITH CHOSEN?

Why did he get the job, over others who in many respects may have been smarter or perhaps better "qualified"? He thought about that a lot through the years. His first answer is probably that he still doesn't know completely. On paper, the other candidates were significantly better educated at more prestigious schools. But here's what the President told Smith later. Lyndon Johnson wanted someone he could trust completely, someone who had useful skills and attributes, like discretion, a bias for action, and perhaps most importantly, someone he couldn't scare off as he had just tried to do. As he well knew, the Marines had already taken care of that last item. Haywood had been yelled at and otherwise dressed down by the best of them.

❝ Colonel Smith, it was a pleasure to meet you. Thank you for your thoughtfulness. ❞

Hussein bin Talal, King of Jordan

44 MY BEST DAY

THE NEW WHITE HOUSE JOB

Haywood found himself at the guest house at the LBJ Ranch. His chief job assignment was to accompany the President any time he left a fixed command structure, such as, the White House, and carry the briefcase containing the codes necessary to launch a nuclear strike should that become necessary. Thankfully, President Johnson never needed to use it.

A military pilot by profession with both fixed wing and rotary aircraft type ratings, Smith found himself as pilot, and often a passenger, on the various aircraft used to transport the President. A Sikorsky "Marine 1" helicopter used to ferry the President on short hops, a customized Lockheed V.C.-140B Jetstar executive jet for trips into short-field airports like the one on his ranch, and the two larger modified Boeing 707s used for longer trips. Although Johnson referred to the Jetstar as Air Force One-Half, all of the aircraft were commonly known as "Air Force One" whenever the President was aboard, which was frequently.

During his term in office, President Johnson logged 523,000 miles aboard the big Boeings alone. Haywood was with him for much of it and can assure you that those aircraft were much more spartan and nowhere near as secure as the modified B-747s available to US Presidents today. By the way, the JetStar Haywood often flew is displayed at the Lyndon B. Johnson National Historical Park.

Haywood was also assigned a fairly broad portfolio of administrative duties including the processing of military commendations, promotions, and assignments; coordinating the use of various government aircraft "At times it felt like I was running a small airline", serving as White House liaison to a seemingly never-ending string of dignitaries and whatever else anyone with the last name of Johnson wanted done. The President and First Lady were very considerate of him, as are their now adult daughters, Luci Baines Johnson, and Lynda Bird Johnson Robb whose children he occasionally looked after when they were quite young.

In fact, upon reflection, that was one of the truly fulfilling aspects of his job. President Johnson was extremely proud of two things: His grandchildren, and

This was a reception the President hosted to honor a Medal of Honor recipient.

His son won the Presidents favor.

I was at a cocktail party for the staff, visiting with Lynda Bird Johnson.

his dogs and the fact that he and the First Family entrusted Haywood to keep an eye on one of those cohorts, the diaper-clad two-legged variety... that was special. Haywood said, "I've got three kids of my own, now fully grown, but when someone else entrusts you, even for a few minutes with their little ones, that's different. If there is anything that will warm the heart of a hardened Marine quicker than a baby or young child, I don't know what it is."

THE CAN DO MAN

In 2024, Lynda Bird Johnson Robb remembers:

"We loved Haywood! Daddy called him a *Can Do Man*. Haywood found a way to get it done. I was very fond of him. I still am."

"The one thing that I will never forget is that Chuck and I were in Law School at the University of Virginia. I had two very young children. That's when I received the message from Mother that my father had died. The next thing I knew, I received a message from Haywood saying that President Nixon was going to send a plane to Charlottesville to pick us up to go to Texas. We rushed to the airport and there was Haywood in the Jetstar. It was very kind of President Nixon and I suspect Haywood had something to do with it, too. This news was a terrible shock to me. It was Haywood's personal touch that made the trip bearable. The fact that he came himself is something I'll always remember."

"Haywood remembers his friends and cares about them, including us right up until this very day."

> **❝ Haywood is part of our family. We love him! ❞**
>
> *Lynda Bird Johnson Robb,*
> *Luci Baines Johnson*

"The baby here is Lucinda. Chuck (my husband) went to Vietnam. Meanwhile, I was receiving his letters. Haywood was helpful in getting my cookies to him. Not just me, but everyone in the White House who had a relative in Vietnam.

When I would see Daddy sometimes I just dropped Lucinda off with Haywood. And sometimes I just came to see him and let him see Lucinda. My Father was very proud of Haywood.

As she grew older, she made the rounds to visit everybody at the White House. I have some lovely photos of her playing in the Lincoln Room."

Lynda Bird Johnson Robb

“ If there is anything that will warm the heart of a hardened Marine quicker than a baby, I don't know what it is. ”

I had the delight of taking my whole family
to the ranch in 2021.

You look at this and you think it's a nice picture,
but he's really chewing me out for something.

MEANWHILE, BACK AT THE RANCH . . .

THE PRESIDENT'S OASIS

President Johnson was a good-hearted man. But it didn't take long to learn that he wasn't always the easiest man in the world to work for or be around. He was demanding, headstrong, a little unreasonable at times, and seldom apologetic. Yet, the President showed time and again that he had it in him to be a real champion at cleaning up his messes. Maybe it was the politician in him. Sometimes inspired by Lady Bird, he had a way of making up for some of the tough talk and oversized expectations by showing, often when you least expected it, that he really cared about you. But Haywood recalled that, "this wasn't that day."

"We had gone to the ranch to… well, to get out of Washington. The ranch was the President's Oasis and, with all due respect to the White House, it was his home. The Kennedys have Hyannis Port, the Bushes, Kennebunkport and the Crawford ranch, Jimmy Carter had his Plains, Georgia farm, and President Johnson had the LBJ ranch. Treating it more like a hotel, they all just borrowed the White House from the American people during their stay in Washington. It's a special place, to be sure, but that doesn't make it home. President Johnson loved the Ranch. He'd rather be there than any place on earth. While other presidents wanted to go on golf trips, Johnson wanted to go to the Ranch. So, I got to know the Ranch pretty well."

Set in the Texas hill country midway between Johnson City and Luckenbach, the ranch has its own paved 6,300 ft. runway, technologically enabled, making it well suited to the Jetstar which brought him there some 74 times during his presidency.

They never took the President's bullet proof limousine to the Ranch. He usually drove his golf cart around. He had cattle, horses, other animals from time to time, a wide array of wildlife and a variety of crops. They used his barn for meetings or to watch a movie. If he wanted to see a movie, he'd call the studio and they'd send him the film.

This is my staff in my office at the White House.

Sally is in the front.

President Johnson paid us a visit.

52 MY BEST DAY

SALLY SNYDER NEUBAUER – WORKING WITH HAYWOOD

Sally Snyder worked as a secretary for Haywood Smith at the White House.

"I first met Haywood when I was working at the West Wing. I had just started working there and we were planning a trip for the President. I was sitting in the meeting taking notes. Haywood and others were there, too. Later, one of the people, he was called the advance man, in the meeting asked what I thought about Haywood."

"I told him I thought he was very professional and got along well with people of all levels. Haywood was very popular at the White House."

Haywood's office was in the East Wing along with the Secret Service. "I always tried to get to the office early because the military people always got there early. I quickly learned that Haywood dealt with personnel at the highest level. The pace was fast, and Haywood was great to work with."

Sally still has his calendar of events for the last three months of his assignment at the White House. From a macro perspective, each day's events show his arrival at "the office" around 9:30am, a line-item detail of the 10 - 30 activities he engaged in each day, and a time of departure whenever it happened.

Haywood reflected, "Without a doubt, Sally was a Godsend. She kept me apprised of what was upcoming, who was looking for time and attention and why. Also, who needed a little consoling or a little straight talk, who I might have offended and needed to apologize to, that is, if she hadn't already handled the apology herself."

"Let me suggest one thing right now. People who do jobs like Sally's don't get near enough respect, appreciation, or money, period."

As a representative sample, Haywood's calendar for 10/1/68 lists 23 agenda items between his arrival at 10:15am and departure for Andrews Air Force Base - home of the Presidential aircraft at 5:10pm to join POTUS on a trip to Saint Louis. Those items consisted of:

- 8 Outbound Phone Calls to mostly military members and contractors for a variety of business purposes

My responsibilities ranged from escorting the President on trips, organizing the flight arrangements for the White House and helping make presentations of medals and awards.

54 MY BEST DAY

- 11 Inbound Phone Calls from mostly military members, media, and private individuals
- 1 Interview with a job prospect
- 1 Meeting out of office
- 2 Calls regarding social plans, one involved World Series tickets
- Three of the items involved coordination of travel and/or use of federal air assets.

His duty day was about 12 hours in total, which was not uncommon.

Sally's desk was right outside of Haywood's office. She worked closely with him and handled a great deal of the President's, and therefore, Haywood's travel plans.

"Sally protected me," he said. "She knew who needed to see me and who didn't."

> **❝ I quickly learned that Haywood dealt with personnel at the highest level. The pace was fast, and Haywood was great to work with. ❞**

I'm sure that's the President on the other end of the line, chewing me out for something.

56 MY BEST DAY

PRESIDENTIAL HEADACHES

One day he was called to the President's Living Quarters. The President was not happy with something Haywood had done. He came back about a half hour later and closed the door. Sally wondered what happened.

She looked at Bill Gully, the Chief of Staff, who had been a Sergeant Major in the Marines at Cherry Point, N.C. whom Haywood recommended.

"I wonder what's going on," Bill said, as he walked into Haywood's office. After a few minutes, he came out laughing.

Sally asked him what happened, and he said Haywood got chewed out for something that the President didn't like. He told Haywood, "You could screw up a two-car funeral!"

There was a couch outside of Haywood's office and at least three desks. One day, Haywood came out and laid down on the couch. He asked for a sheet of paper. He drew a picture on it. It was an oblong shaped figure. He said, "Would you take this over to Dr. Burkley's office and get me one of these pills? It looks like this."

After 50 years, Sally summed it up. "Working with Haywood was great. He always treated everyone in the office with great respect and fairness."

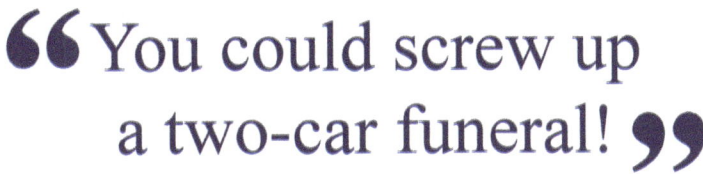

❝ You could screw up a two-car funeral! ❞

I revisited my old office on the ranch 50 years later. What memories it brought back. From this vantage point, I saw leaders from all over the world come to visit President Johnson.

This photo was taken by the Presidential photographer, Okamoto. You can see the ranch's reflection in my sunglasses.

MEANWHILE BACK AT THE RANCH . . .

THE TIME HAYWOOD MADE THE PRESIDENT GO BLIND

Haywood had two offices. One in the White House and one at the Ranch.

"Every day at the Ranch was different for me. We never knew what to expect, so we expected everything. It might be to pick up some congressmen at Bergstrom Air Force Base. It might be to fly a celebrity in from another airport. It could be to determine why Lady Bird's flowers around the runway were dying. I never knew."

Notable visitors to the Ranch included President Richard M. Nixon, Texas Governor John Connelly, President Harry S Truman, President John F. Kennedy, Reverend Billy Graham, Mexico President Gustavo Diaz Ordaz, George McGovern, Colorado Senator and Presidential Candidate, and West German Chancellor Konrad Adenauer.

An example of each day's unusual activity happened during Haywood's first year with the President. He answered the phone in his office. It was the President, THE President. "Yes Mr. President."

"Major!" he practically screamed, with that twangy Texas drawl. "You're causing me to go blind! Get off my ranch!" Click.

"President Johnson never struggled with convincing you that he wasn't happy about something."

Haywood sat at his desk staring at the phone, trying to figure out how he got here, and what would happen next.

At the moment, he was a 33 year-old Marine officer who was not a graduate of the US Naval Academy but had come up through Memphis State with a bachelor's degree, average grades, and some pretty good piloting skills. He had somehow vaulted over stiff competition from the different service branches, and found himself at the White House, working daily with then, the most powerful man on the planet, President Lyndon Baines Johnson (LBJ).

Previously serving as Vice President to President John F. Kennedy, Mr. Johnson's life changed radically on November 22, 1963, when he ascended to

One of my duties was to assist Jim Cross in flying Air Force One. This was especially helpful during overseas flights.

Jim and I became good friends over the years of working together.

the presidency upon President Kennedy's sudden death in Dallas at the hands of Lee Harvey Oswald.

"I didn't know what to do or why he was mad. I was about to go see him when the doctor came out of the ranch house and into my little office. He explained that the President had been riding around in his cart and got a spec of dirt in his eye. Of course, he blamed me. The doctor said he'd be fine and not to worry about it. So I waited a few hours and when no one came to yank me out of my chair, I decided the doctor was right."

"I saw the President later that day. He said, 'I guess you heard about what happened.'"

"Yes sir."

"Well, what are you going to do about it?"

"About you getting dust in your eyes?"

"Yes. I don't want that to happen again."

"I don't know, Mr. President, but I'll think of something."

"Of course, I had no idea how to prevent dust on the road. But eventually, I came up with a plan."

Haywood secured a water truck from Bergstrom Air Force Base and hired several local Hispanic workers. Whenever word came that the President was going to take a drive, the "Dirt Patrol" jumped into action. They would spray the dirt road to prevent dust and dirt particles hitting the President.

"It was something to see. Those guys took their job seriously. When they received a call, they jumped on the truck and flew out of the garage like firemen going to a fire."

I DON'T CARE WHAT YOU HAD FOR BREAKFAST

Najeeb Halaby was the administrator of the FAA. He said The President shouldn't ride around with Dale Meeks, who flew the King Air, as his pilot at the Ranch. "He's a civilian and shouldn't be the only pilot in the cockpit.

> **❝** It was my great pleasure to meet you, Haywood, at my home on the occasion of my birthday. I'm glad President Johnson introduced you to me. You are always welcome back. **❞**

Harry Truman, President

This signed photo stills hangs in my bedroom. I was really honored to have met President Truman

Haywood needs to learn to fly it, too."

So, one day, Haywood was sitting on a fence rail outside the Ranch when Halaby and the President drove up purposefully. The President pointed at the King Air and asked, "Haywood can you fly that airplane?"

Haywood answered, "Mr. President, I don't know what type that is, or whether I've ever flown one exactly like it. But I have flown all types of prop planes and small jets."

"Whoa-whoa-whoa-whoa," the President said. "I don't care what you had for breakfast. I just want to know if you can fly the plane."

"Yes sir. I can fly it," Haywood answered.

The President looked at Najeeb and said, "I told you he could."

They drove off.

TRUMAN'S BIRTHDAY

"We were coming back from somewhere and the President said, 'I want to stop by and see President Truman. It's his birthday.'"

Landing in Kansas, they drove to Truman's house. LBJ got out, the Secret Service got out. And Okamoto, the President's photographer got out. Haywood stayed in the car.

"In a few minutes. a Secret Service agent came and told me the President wanted to see me."

Haywood entered the house where Johnson introduced him to Truman, "Mr. President, this is Major Smith. He told me that you were his favorite President and I thought maybe you'd like to give him an autographed photo."

Truman said, "I certainly would!"

Haywood still has the autographed photo displayed on the wall in his bedroom.

"Of course, I would have received more mileage if I had told President Johnson that *he* was my favorite President."

> **❝ Haywood, it was an honor to have made your acquaintance. I hope we will see each other again. ❞**
>
> *Mahatma Gandhi, President, Republic of India.*

Luci's dog Freckles, was the pup of the President's dog, Him.

President Johnson loved his pups!

PRESIDENT JOHNSON PLAYS GOLF

The President needed a warm climate to recuperate from gall bladder surgery. So, they got in Air Force One and flew to an island in Central America. The plans were to stay for three weeks, even though Haywood had never seen him stay in one place for more than a week.

The second day there, an agent from the Secret Service asked, "Does anybody play golf." Smith said that he did. Yoichi Okamoto, the presidential photographer, said he did. So did Pat Nugent, the President's future son-in-law, Luci's husband.

"Okay, the President wants to play golf," the agent said.

"I didn't know that the President played golf. I never saw him play and never heard him talk about golf. We were all in different carts. The Secret Service was driving the President's cart."

"So, we got to the first tee. Okamoto hit a pretty good shot. Pat hit a pretty good shot. I hit a really long drive. The President had teed off first and as a matter of fact, he hit several balls. None of them went farther than 30 yards. He got in the cart and went to the farthest ball, which happened to be mine, and he played that one. The rest of them hit their own balls, except for me. My ball was now the one hit 30 yards away from the tee. After we hit our second shots, the President had the Secret Service drive up to the green and played the ball closest to the pin."

"He did that for four holes, and then he quit. On every hole, he played the best ball. He wasn't much of a golfer. But then again that may have been his first time to play. That's the only time I ever saw him swing a club."

THE ATTACK OF FRECKLES

Haywood went to visit the President's daughter, Luci, in Austin. As mentioned, she married Pat Nugent, who became Haywood's good friend. They knew he was coming to Texas, so they invited him for dinner. Pat told him he wanted to play golf beforehand.

When they came back to the house, Luci came running out, crying. Pat asked

Most people know the Secret Service protects the President, few people realize what the Military Aides do.

If you asked me to tell you what the job was, I'd have to say, "whatever he told me to do."

her what the matter was. "I was cooking chicken and I got everything set on the table, ready for you to walk in. I went back in the kitchen and the chicken was gone. The dog had taken off with it." That little beagle, Freckles, that was the son of the President's dog, Him, had jumped up in the chair, onto the table, then outside in the backyard to enjoy his feast.

Haywood laughed and recalled, "So, we ordered pizza."

TELL'EM *YOU'RE* STUPID

Mrs. Johnson and Haywood were standing in the President's office at the Ranch watching him shuffling through some papers. He was looking for the name of an Assistant Secretary he had appointed. He looked up and asked, "Who is that guy I nominated?"

Haywood said, "I don't know, Mr. President."

"Well call somebody and find out."

"Yes sir." He picked up the phone and asked for the Secretary of the Navy. When he was connected, he said, "I'm calling from the President's Office and the President wants to know-"

The President pushed the dial down and promptly disconnected the call. Haywood looked up at him for an explanation.

"Look, Haywood, don't tell'em I'm stupid. Tell'em *you're* stupid!"

LBJ THE COMEDIAN

"The President didn't like the press being on the ranch as much as they were there. And he enjoyed playing a prank on them from time to time," Haywood remembers.

"Someone had given him the prettiest deer you've ever seen. It was a big one, too. In fact, we had to build the fence higher to keep him from jumping over it. Well, that deer liked tobacco. So, one day when the press was there, the President asked if anybody in the Secret Service had any cigarettes. Somebody gave him a few and he broke the tobacco into little pieces."

❝Thank you, Haywood, for transporting me to Camp David to speak at the Sunday services. What a joy to get to know you! I may steal some of your stories. Don't tell.**❞**

Billy Graham, evangelist

"He took several of the ladies in the Press Corp on a tour of the Ranch in his jeep. When he got to where the deer was, he stopped, gave them some tobacco, and told them to feed the deer and the White House photographer, Okamoto, would take their photo. They did and while they were feeding the deer, it proceeded to pee all over them. What they didn't know and what the President did know was that somehow the tobacco made the deer pee. Have you ever seen a deer pee? It resembles a yard sprinkler, going back and forth. He laughed harder than maybe I had ever seen him laugh. He made sure he wasn't in the picture."

"He was more of a comedian than most people knew. He had a boat on the Ranch that was also a car. He kept it on a part of the Ranch called, of all things, The Haywood Place. I never did learn why it was named that, but I do know it had that name before I ever got there. It took about 10 minutes to get to the lake by helicopter. He would ask his guests to get in, what they assumed was a car. Then, as he'd take them on a tour, he would suddenly drive right into the lake. There were a lot of screams during that prank."

MR. SAM AT THE BORDER

"Sam was the President's brother, and he was a pistol. He was very hard to keep up with."

"We were on the Ranch and the President needed to go back to Washington. Of course, I went with him."

"I received a call from Sam, who said, *I'm down here at Cousin Oriole's Place*, which was on the Ranch. *I need to get a car to pick me up.*"

"So, I sent a car and went back to watching the football game. That game finished and I watched another."

"About three hours after that call, the phone rang again, and it was Sam's driver. *I thought I better call and tell you that we're here at the Mexican Border and we're about to go across. I don't know if I'm supposed to do that or not.*"

"I couldn't believe what I had heard. Sam had somehow talked the driver into taking him to the Mexican border. After telling him not to enter Mexico, I

immediately called the Secret Service and they brought him back."

"The President would have killed us if Mr. Sam had crossed the Border and got into trouble. He would have sent me south of the Border himself!"

JEANNIE AT THE HOSPITAL

When Jeannie was in the hospital with cancer, the President got wind of it and called Haywood who was in his White House office. "I hear Jeannie is in the hospital."

"Yes sir."

"Where?"

"Millington, Tennessee."

"Haywood, you go get in the Jet-Star and fly to Millington and go be with her."

"Yes sir, Mr. President."

A car picked him up and took him to the hospital. He was met at Jeannie's door by a Navy Captain. He said, "I want you to understand what happened. The Commander got a call. And he asked, "Who's calling?"

"The President."

"The president of what?"

"The President of the United States. I want you to send Jeannie Smith to Bethesda Hospital and I want the best doctors in this country to take care of her. We've got this in process right now."

Haywood was very touched by the President's gesture, and said, "I see. Let's wait until I talk to Jeannie."

He talked to Jeannie and told her, but she wanted to stay where she was.

So, Haywood told the Captain, "She doesn't want to go. Call Washington and tell them to cancel that aircraft. I appreciate your work on her behalf."

The surgery went well, and she got to go home.

"That's why I was always so loyal to President Johnson. He chewed me out many a time, but he also would do anything for Jeannie and me. In fact, the next day the whole room was covered in flowers by the time I got there. The flowers

❝ I needed to go to South America to speak at a judicial conference. Haywood flew with us in the President's plane. That started a relationship that's lasted a lifetime. My wife made him a pie for Christmas. ❞

Chief Justice Earl Warren

were from the President and Mrs. Johnson."

"I knew the President really cared about me and my family. President Johnson never would admit or say he was wrong, but he would also do something in the future that made things 100% better."

THE CHIEF JUSTICE AND HAYWOOD IN BOLIVIA

Chief Justice Earl Warren wrote a letter to the President saying that he was going to Bolivia for the World Court and he'd like to have an airplane. The President said he wanted him to go in Air Force One and he wanted Haywood to go with him.

"The Chief Justice brought his wife and his son who was a judge. That was it. We landed in LaPaz, 5,000 feet above sea level. The Chief Justice deplaned, and we had to give him an oxygen mask because of the altitude. But he was able to get acclimated and enjoyed the trip."

"His wife asked who was washing my clothes. I told her that I would wash them myself. She said, Give me those clothes, and then she washed them for me. Mrs. Warren and I got to be great friends. She always wanted to have her photo made with me. For some reason, she wanted me to wear a hat in the photos. They were pretty silly but she loved it."

"When we got back, the Chief Justice wrote a thoughtful note about my help to the President. The President called me in and read the letter. Then he said, 'Why don't you act like that when you're around me?'"

"About Christmas time, a messenger came in and gave me a pecan pie with a note of thanks from Justice Warren's wife."

HAYWOOD GETS THROWN UNDER THE BUS

A representative for Howard Hughes came to the Ranch to see the President. He wanted to talk to the President about new routes for Air West.

The President was also scheduled to meet Russell Brown, an old friend and classmate of Johnson's. The President said, "Don't let Mr. Brown land until I

> **"The President would make up for throwing him under the bus. He always did."**

As I was bringing the President of Mexico from the airport to the White House, he asked me where we were going to land. "In the front yard," I said.

finish with my current meeting. I don't want them here at the same time."

Haywood then got a call from Brown's pilot saying they were 20 minutes out. Haywood relayed that information to the President.

The President said, "I don't want him landing right now."

So, Haywood called the pilot back and said, "The airfield is not ready for landing right now. I'll call you back in about 15 minutes and give you an estimated time to land."

He finally told them to land at Bergstrom Air Force Base and told them that he would be there in a helicopter to pick him up. When Mr. Brown came onboard, he asked why they couldn't land at the Ranch. Haywood explained that due to circumstances beyond his control, their big plane couldn't land at this time and that's why he would have to pick him up in the helicopter.

Meanwhile, the other guest left.

Mr Brown was mad. When he got to see the President, Brown said, "Lyndon, who in the hell is Major Smith?"

"Why?"

"I've been all over Texas waiting to get here but Major Smith wouldn't let me land. I could have been here an hour ago."

The President responded, "I cannot believe that. Sometimes we just have people here who are not very capable."

When Brown was leaving, the President called Haywood aside and apologized to him. Haywood told him that was okay. He knew the President would make up for throwing him under the bus. He always did.

YOU KILLED MY FLOWERS!

One day when Haywood was at the Ranch, the President called him and said, "Haywood, you've killed all the wildflowers!"

The President believed that the jet exhaust from the planes that landed only a few times a day was killing Lady Bird's Blue Bonnets. Haywood knew better than to argue, so he just said, "Yes Mr. President."

General Clifton and I were pinning a promotion on a Lt. Colonel.

"Well, what are you going to do about it?" LBJ demanded.

He stuttered around and said, "We'll water them more."

The President seemed satisfied

"That wasn't my job, but I didn't point that out. It was typical of the kind of things the President expected me to add to my growing list of responsibilities."

NOT WELCOME AT THE RANCH

Haywood reported to General Clifton, but the President didn't like him. Johnson called him into his office and told him, "Now, I don't want that General coming down to the Ranch. I don't want him getting in my business."

"Yes sir, Mr. President."

That was a difficult assignment since he was a General and Haywood's boss. Then the General wrote a memorandum to the President. Marie, the President's secretary read it, called, and said, "Haywood, you don't want the President to read this."

He said, "Read what?"

She said, "The General sent a memorandum to the President. You know how he feels about that. He's not going to like this."

Haywood went over and picked it up and walked over to the General's office. "General, this memo..." He started.

The General interrupted and said, "Where did you get that from?"

"I got it from Marie."

"Who is she?"

"She's the President's secretary."

He said, "You take that back to her and tell her that I said to put it in the President's night reading."

Haywood complied. Marie said, "Haywood you know the President isn't going

to like this."

It wasn't long before LBJ called him into his office again. He was holding the memorandum. "What is this?"

"Well, Mr. President, he told me to give it to you, and he's a General so I had to obey orders."

The President looked at him with his piercing look that he was famous for. Then he said, "You better not let him on the Ranch."

But as fate would have it, one day the General showed up, unannounced, on the courier plane that daily brought the correspondence from the White House.

Smith asked him what he was doing there and the General said that, as he understood it, the Ranch was part of his responsibility so, he should take a look around. The General wanted Haywood to give him a tour. About that time, the President rounded the corner in his golf cart and saw the Colonel.

He called Smith over and said, "I told you that I didn't want him down here. What don't you understand about what I told you?"

"Yes sir, but I couldn't tell a General what to do."

So, three or four days after that, Haywood was back in the White House. The General had a large office and the assistant aides had smaller ones, in front of his. Haywood noticed the lights were on in the General's office. He asked him what he was doing there so early.

The General said, "I just got a call saying they have a very, very important job for me at the Pentagon and they needed me immediately to take care of it." Haywood never saw him again.

THE SURPRISE AT PERCY PRIEST DAM

One day the President came over to see him in his little office. He glanced at the painting on the wall. It was of him. Smith learned later from Rufus Youngblood, a Secret Service agent, that the President said, "See, he had my picture up in his office."

❝ What a joy and surprise to sit beside you at the dedication of Percy Priest Dam. When the President called you to stand by him and promoted you to Colonel, it was clear that you were as surprised as anyone else. ❞

Buford Ellington, Governor, Tennessee

While President Johnson was still in Haywood's modest office, he asked, "Do you think you can handle this thing?" He was talking about the General's job as Armed Forces Aide.

"Yes sir."

He turned around and walked out.

During a week-long leave period, Haywood received a call from the White House instructing him to report back immediately. Upon asking why, he was told that General Clifton, the Armed Forces Aide had submitted his retirement papers, and he was to be his replacement.

A few weeks later, the President was going to fly down to dedicate the new Percy Priest Dam in Nashville. Haywood had arranged for another officer to go. Then, the Executive Assistant to the President called and said, "The President wants you to go." So, he did.

Before leaving, Smith called his relatives who lived in the area and told them, "After we land, and the motorcade gets away, you can come on board Air Force One and I'll give you the tour." He knew the President would be on stage giving a speech so he wouldn't be needed during that time.

After Air Force One landed, the motorcade was ready to go and he knew his relatives were ready for their tour. Then he received a call from Youngblood, the Secret Service agent. "The motorcade is about ready to go. Aren't you coming?"

Smith told him that he was going to stay on the plane and show some relatives around. Then he got a call from Lem, another Secret Service agent. "The President wants you in the motorcade."

So, Haywood had to wave goodbye to his relatives. Upon reaching the new dam, the President sat down on the stage. Smith stood in the back, with "The Football" and the President's doctor. Then a Secret Service agent came over to him and said, "The President wants you to sit on stage."

He was mystified even more when LBJ motioned for him to sit between Tennessee Governor Buford Ellington and him. Buford was a friend of Smith's and said, "Haywood, it's good to see you. What are you doing here on stage?"

“If I'd known you were going to get such a big head, I'd have announced it somewhere else.”

"I have no idea."

He looked out in the audience and saw six generals who were in the Engineering Corp that built the dam. So, he decided the President just wanted him up there to represent the military.

The President stood, went to the podium, and said, "Before I dedicate this dam, I have an important announcement to make." Haywood leaned forward a little. He wasn't aware of an announcement, so he decided it was late-breaking news.

He continued, "In the history of the United States, this country has never had a Marine as the Armed Forces Aide to the President. I have decided to have a Marine Colonel to fill that position."

Haywood didn't have any idea who he was talking about.

LBJ continued, "And today I'm promoting him from Lieutenant Colonel to Colonel." Well, Haywood knew that surely couldn't be him, as many times as he had chewed him out.

"Haywood Smith, come up here."

So, Lieutenant Colonel Haywood Smith walked up and stood beside the President. "I was completely dumbfounded. Even then, I thought I was called up to help make the presentation to the new Armed Forces Aide. But the President shook my hand. It was me!"

The entire White House staff clapped loud and long because they knew him. Even the White House Press cheered. He was so proud, and rightfully so. Then President Johnson leaned closer to the Colonel and said, "Sit down."

When they got back in Air Force One, Haywood walked back to him and said, "Mr. President, I'm going to justify your appointment by doing the very best job I can."

"President Johnson looked up at me and said, 'I know that, but if I'd known you were going to get such a big head, I'd have announced it somewhere else'."

" Looks like we're going to have a good day. "

CARRYING "THE FOOTBALL"

The Armed Forces Aide was with the President a great deal of the time and therefore was generally assigned to carry the briefcase called "The Football."

That was several decades ago, and things have changed significantly. Still, it's very interesting to learn what was in the mysterious briefcase.

"There was a black book and a yellow book. They were for different nuclear missile targets. Military, domestic, and manufacturing targets.

"There were also large rolls of nickels, dimes, and quarters in the bag. It was explained to me that if the President happened to be out anywhere, he could stop at a phone booth, use that change, and reach whoever needed to be contacted."

Just as essential, Haywood carried a secret weapon that was not in that bag. It enabled him to open a lot of doors, remove barriers, and change people's priorities, if not their minds, with five simple words, "The President wants this done." He viewed it as his sacred option and was judicious about using it. No one ever chose to find out if he was bluffing.

"THE FOOTBALL" GOES TO CHURCH

As already noted, the Colonel's job was to accompany the President whenever he left the confines of the White House, be it a trip around the world, or something as simple as going to church, which the Johnsons did frequently. In those cases, with his trusty companion, "The Football," the Colonel tagged along. As a result, he heard many long sermons, a variety of songs, and shared some lunches with very important people.

Even when they went to Camp David for the weekend, a preacher often came out to hold service. The Reverend Billy Graham was a regular. When he came to visit, Haywood would meet him at the airport to ensure his transportation and accommodation.

One Sunday as the Johnsons were headed to church, Haywood was riding up front with the Secret Service and LBJ and Lady Bird were in the back.

> **“Colonel Smith, thank you for your consistent help as I visited numerous times with the President.”**
>
> *J. Edgar Hoover*

Smith looked over at the Secret Service driver and asked, "How are we doing?" The agent looked at him, smiled and said, "Looks like we're going to have a good day."

About that time, they heard Lady Bird say, "Honey, give me some money for collection."

The President was quiet and didn't respond. So, she spoke up again, "Honey, I need some money before we go into church so I can put something in the collection plate."

The President said, "Lady Bird, use your own money."

Haywood looked at the agent and said, "It's *not* going to be a good day."

HOOVER'S ADVICE TO KEEP SECRETS FROM THE SECRET SERVICE

One day the President was talking to J. Edgar Hoover, the Director of the FBI. "If you didn't tell everybody where you're going," the Director said, "you wouldn't have all those Secret Service guys around you, because they wouldn't know where you were going."

The President thought about that. Two days later, he called Haywood and said, "Get Air Force One ready to go."

"Yes sir. Where are we going?"

"I'll let you know."

"Yes sir."

The Colonel called Jim Cross, the lead pilot for Air Force One, and told him the President wanted them to get Air Force One ready.

"Where are we going?"

"He's going to let us know."

"I've got to know where we're going, Haywood. I've got to file a flight plan."

He said, "Well, he's not telling me. How do I know where we're going?"

On Opening Day, April 9, 1965, a sold-out crowd of 47,879 watched an exhibition game between the Houston Astros and the New York Yankees. President Lyndon B. Johnson and his wife Lady Bird were in attendance, as well as Texas Governor John Connally and Houston Mayor Louie Welch. Governor Connally tossed out the first ball for the first game ever played indoors. Dick "Turk" Farrell of the Astros threw the first pitch. Mickey Mantle had both the first hit (a single) and the first home run in the Astrodome. The Astros beat the Yankees that night, 2–1.

President Johnson stopped at the Astrodome that evening en route to his home in Johnson City and paid his respects to baseball and Astros president Roy Hofheinz. He and Lady Bird watched the opening night game from behind the glass in Judge Hofheinz's private box high in right field just to the right of the giant scoreboard. LBJ ate hors d'œuvres and chicken and ice cream while watching the game. "Roy, I want to congratulate you; it shows so much imagination," he was heard to say. Later, he called the stadium "massive" and "beautiful." Although the president's visit overshadowed all others, dignitaries swarmed through the "Eighth Wonder of the World" during the three days of the exhibition series and for opening night against the Phillies on April 12. Chris Short of the Phillies shut out the Astros on four hits, with 12 strikeouts.

So, as they were heading to the airport and Haywood asked, "Mr. President . . . where are we going?"

"I'll let you know."

"He didn't have any idea all the work it required when the President of the United States left Washington in Air Force One. Support Staff must meet him. Transportation has to be arranged. The Secret Service has to be there before he's there. There are tons of things that must be done."

So, they board Air Force One and Cross again asks, "Where are we going?"

Haywood went back and asked, "Mr. President, What's our destination?"

"I'll let you know when we get airborne."

Trying to think of what to say next, Haywood asked, "Well, which *direction* should we go?"

Johnson said, "Head West."

"Yes sir."

"Just kind of head toward the Ranch. We may go there."

Haywood told Cross, "I don't know. He said just head toward the Ranch."

Then the President called him back and said, "And we might go to Houston. They are opening the Astrodom Roy Hofheinz had served as a Texas state representative, the mayor of Houston, a county judge and a wealthy real estate developer. He was the driving force in the building of the Astrodome.

Haywood went back and told Cross, "I don't know where we're going. He just said to head West.

"So, we're going to the Ranch or the Astrodome, huh?" "Yeah."

Cross just shook his head.

After a bit, Cross spoke up, "Okay, we're at a point where we are either going to the Ranch or to Houston."

Haywood went back again and said, "Mr. President, we've got to know where

> **❝ I became very close to Haywood during and after Lyndon was President. Things lit up when he came for supper. ❞**
>
> *John Connally, Governor, Texas*

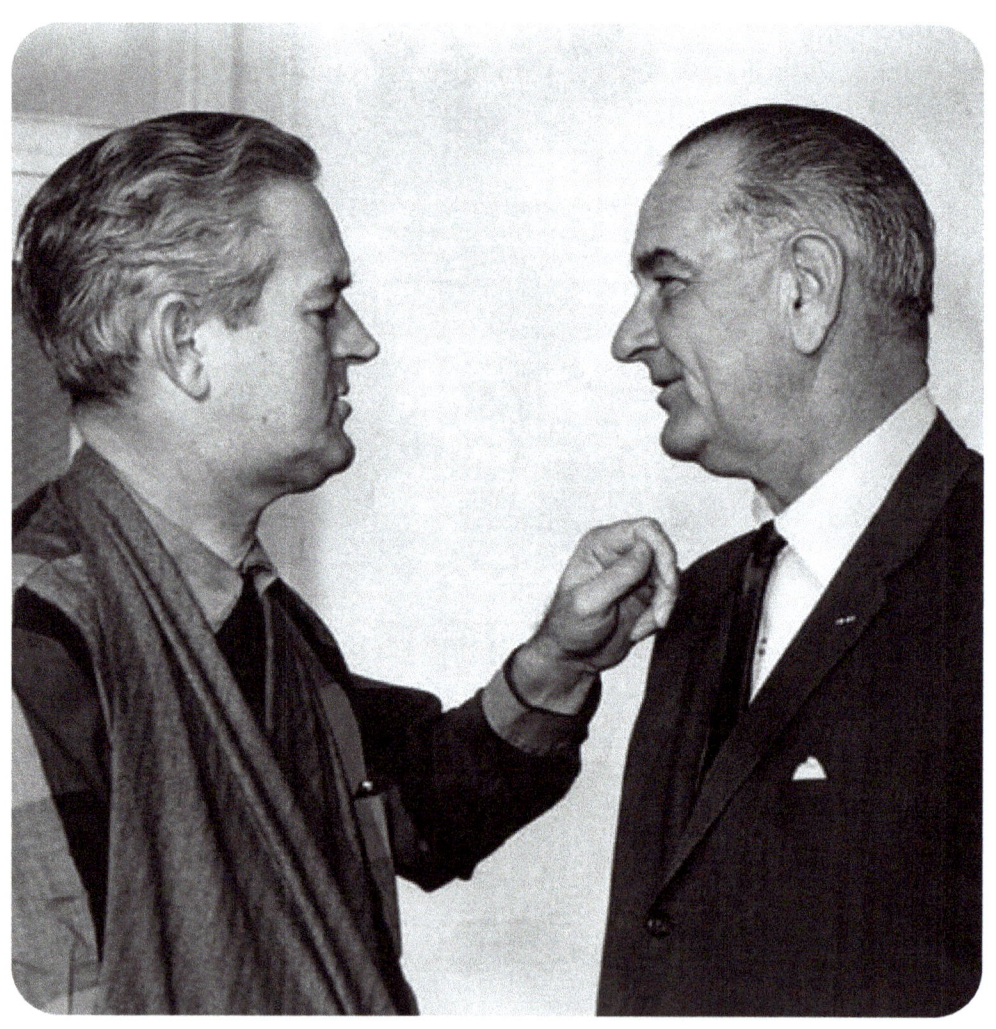

The President and Governor Connally were good friends and enjoyed visits at the ranch.

we're going. We're at that point where we have to head in one direction or the other."

LBJ said. "Let's go see Hofheinz."

"Meanwhile, the Press Plane was following Air Force One. They saw that we were heading West, so they assumed the President was going to the Ranch. The Secret Service was going crazy, trying to accommodate the President with no advance warning that he was going to Houston. Now they learn that he's not just going to Houston, he's going to one of the largest buildings in the United States, with close to 50,000 people in there!"

"The Secret Service quickly arranged transportation, and we arrived at the Astrodome. We sat in Hofheinz's box. The restroom commodes had cowhide for seats!"

"We were sitting in the best seats in the Astrodome and watching a major league ballgame. I was really happy. We had watched about three innings when the President said, 'Let's go.'"

"So, back in the cars we go. The Secret Service was once again scrambling. We were about halfway back to the airport when we met a long line of cars heading in the opposite direction. It was the Press Corp. They had landed at Bergstrom in Austin to go the Ranch and got word that the President went to the Astrodome. So, they got back in their plane, flew to Houston, and were on their way to the game."

"The President liked that more than anything I had ever seen. We flew to the Ranch. Just another day with President Johnson."

GOVERNOR CONNALLY

John Connally threw out the first pitch at the first game in the Astrodome. The Governor and the President were very good friends. As a matter of fact, Governor Connally was the most frequent guest at the Ranch. He could have been President at one time.

When the Governor came to the Ranch, he and the President would talk politics all day. They'd drive around in the golf cart down in the pasture, on the runway,

> **❝** Haywood, we really enjoyed our time in your office while we waited to meet the President. Come see us. Maybe we'll give you a ride. **❞**
>
> *Frank Borman, James Lovell, Willian Anders, Apollo 8 Mission astronauts*

> **❝** Haywood has been a great friend. I'm glad he didn't continue to pursue his tests to be an astronaut. I might have been bumped! **❞**
>
> *Senator John Glenn, astronaut*

or on the roads in the Ranch.

Connally said of Haywood, "He was a very likable man. I always described him as straight up."

ADVENTURES ON *THE SEQUOIA*

"The President had just taken office and was hosting several high-ranking White House personnel and Cabinet Members on the Presidential yacht, *The Sequoia*. Dean Rusk was speaking. 'We need to get rid of J. Edgar Hoover.' Then the President came in and they addressed the matter with him."

The President leaned back and said, "I don't know, I'd rather have him on the inside peeing out than on the outside peeing in."

The Sequoia was a beautiful vessel. It had been used by Herbert Hoover, Franklin Roosevelt, Harry Truman, Dwight Eisenhower, and John Kennedy. President Johnson's first time on board was in 1949 when he and Mrs. Johnson had been invited to attend a social gathering by Secretary of the Navy, James Forrestal. Since then, he was part of several meetings there, including many with President Kennedy.

The yacht also had a screen to watch movies. President Johnson enjoyed floating down the Potomac, watching a movie. It was a good way to unwind while he was in Washington.

"We were watching *Guess Who's Coming to Dinner?* The President was able to watch the latest movies by having someone in his office request them from the production company. In a day or two, he'd have the film reels. He loved to invite his close friends to watch the movie with him."

"As we were watching the movie, we floated by Washington National Airport. The President motioned for me to come where he was sitting and said, 'We can't even hear the movie because of all these jets. Can we do something about that?'"

Colonel Smith knew they had some Secret Service Agents at the airport, so he called and said to the agent that answered, "Stop the jets until we get down the river."

Working close to the President, I got to shake his hand a number of times. But once during a State Dinner, I noticed that the receiving line was near the end, so I got in line. As I shook the President's hand, he said, "Haywood what are you doing?" I said, "I thought I'd shake your hand, too." To that he huffed, "Don't you realize how tired I am of shaking people's hands?"

I never got in line again.

> **When I sat next to Haywood at a State Dinner, I was immediately taken by his charm and gentlemanly manner. I looked over at this marine in uniform and heard myself asking, 'Are you married?'**
>
> *Janet Leigh, actress*

"Says who?" the agent asked.

"The President of the United States."

The agent paused, took the message, and asked, "Uh, okay. How long?"

The Colonel said that he didn't know, but that he would call him back.

They stopped the jets. The President said, "That's better."

The Sequoia continued its cruise along the Potomac as they watched the movie with the President.

Sometime later, Haywood received a call on the boat from the agent. "When can we let them land? They're really stacked up."

Smith told him to let them go.

The next day, Marvin Watson called him. Marvin was the President's advisor and similar to the Chief of Staff. He would later become the Postmaster General. "Haywood, did we hold up planes for the President?"

"Well, we might have held them up for a little while."

"I've received about 20 calls from senators who were on some of those jets, waiting to land."

They never heard any more about it.

PARTIES AT THE WHITE HOUSE

There were many parties, dinners, and other functions at the White House. Sometimes they had them at the White House and sometimes at the Pentagon. "

The President liked for me to attend the State Dinners. Maybe it was because of the uniform."

"I remember one time, sitting right between Janet Leigh and Wernher von Braun. I thought, This is pretty good. On one side, I'm seated next to the best-looking woman in the world. On my other side is the smartest man in the world. I wonder what they think about me?"

Lady Bird Johnson was a kind and gracious woman.

96 MY BEST DAY

HAYWOOD REMEMBERS LADY BIRD

"The First Lady stayed in the background, but she could handle the President. She was one smart lady, too. Mrs. Johnson helped him make good decisions. She was his most trusted confidant."

"Mrs. Johnson did a great job of decorating the White House for Christmas. She always had a party for the staff. It was a beautiful time."

"She was a very gracious woman and recognized that the President could be a little gruff. She made up for it when she could."

THE FIRST LADY'S FUNERAL

"After President Johnson died, Mrs. Johnson moved to Austin. She died in 2007. I loved her dearly and was honored to attend her funeral. There were flowers everywhere around her home, at the funeral service, and all over both sides of the highway. One of her secret service agents said, If they don't have Blue Bells in Heaven, they're gonna have them now."

"As First Lady, she formed her own committee to undertake what was called 'beautification' but had a wide range of objectives, In Washington, D.C., the committee took on two initiatives — to turn the capital into a 'garden city' with tree-lined streets and flowering parks but also to go beyond the tourist center and add plantings and improve playgrounds in low income neighborhoods."

Lady Bird Johnson's beautification efforts weren't restricted to the Beltway. Her impact on policy continued to resonate throughout Johnson's presidency. PBS's "Lady Bird Johnson: Portrait of a First Lady" quoted the president as telling his staff, "You know I love that woman and she wants that Highway Beautification Act... by God, we're going to get it for her."

(Excerpt from an article by Áine Cain, Business Insider)

I had to coordinate the President's movements with the Secret Service.

> **"** Colonel Smith, it was my privilege to meet you for the second time. Personal regards. **"**
>
> *Charles De Gaulle, President, France*

98 MY BEST DAY

HAYWOOD AND THE SECRET SERVICE

The Colonel decided it wasn't the best time to tell that agent about how the President hated the intrusion of the Secret Service on the ranch. "Look at them," Johnson had said one day while they were looking out his office window. "They look like a bunch of Mexican generals walking around here."

"There were two agents, the head of the Presidential detail, Rufus Youngblood and Lem Johns that he really liked, and they liked him. They would have taken a bullet for him in a minute. Their office was very close to mine."

When Johnson moved, it was important for the Secret Service to know everything about it. They provided all the transportation and security for the President and coordinated all operations with the military. That meant Haywood knew them all by name and they knew him. He was like an agent for them because they were constantly in touch. They depended on him to keep them updated on where the President was going and when they were leaving.

When they traveled, the Colonel was not in uniform, unless it was a military occasion. Otherwise, he would put on a black suit. He wore the same black suit all the time.

"The Secret Service did their best with President Johnson. They might say, Mr. President, we don't want you to go to that location. He would say, Well, that's too bad because that's where I'm going."

"Once he said, If I did everything you (the Secret Service) wanted me to do, you'd be sleeping with me and my wife!"

THE PHOTO WITH CHARLES DE GAULLE

Haywood was with the President at a meeting of leaders of nations. The photographer said, "We're going to take a photo that's going to be a picture for history of all these world leaders. You need to get the President over here on these cathedral steps". So, Smith told the President. He asked what it was for and agreed to be in the photo.

They walked over to the Cathedral and there were the leaders of all these

A GREAT HONOR

On the Kennedy Grave there is the Eternal Flame. Every year, the President of the United States places a Presidential Wreath by the Eternal Flame.

"This year, President Johnson told me to lay the wreath on President Kennedy's grave. This was on President Kennedy's birthday. Several of the Kennedy family were there. It was a true honor."

> **❝** Haywood placed the wreath on Jack's grave at the second anniversary of his assassination. I will always be grateful for that. **❞**
>
> *Jacqueline Kennedy Onnassis*

100 MY BEST DAY

nations. They were on the steps, which were very small, maybe a couple of inches high. The President was standing close to Churchill, and he was standing next to Charles de Gaulle.

"Well, with his top hat on, De Gaulle was taller than the President, who was a tall man himself. I knew that the President didn't like that. Just as the photographer was about to take to take the photo, President Johnson took one step back to that higher step, which made him just as tall as de Gaulle."

PICKING UP ROCKS

One day when Haywood was at the Ranch, the President called him from his office. He said, "Haywood, did you hire those people who are picking up rocks?"

"No sir."

"Well, what are we paying them?"

"I don't know, Mr. President."

"Well, you got a one-armed guy out here. What are we paying him? Maybe we should get him at half-price."

"He paused and laughed, 'He's a good man!'"

SECRETARY VANCE AT CAMP DAVID

Every morning when they were at Camp David, Haywood would brief the President on what had happened overnight. Deputy Secretary of Defense Cyrus Vance was present as he was reporting about activities in Vietnam. Cyrus was a graduate of Yale Law School.

Smith told the President about an unusual event involving an A.D.

"What's an A.D.?"

"It's a prop airplane, Mr. President. It shot down a MIG. That's very unusual. You don't have a prop airplane shoot down a jet very often."

"Well, where did they shoot it down at?"

"I think it was in the northern edge of Vietnam," the Colonel said.

> **❝** He thought somebody was shooting at him with a cannon. It's funny now, but it wasn't funny then. He was some kind of mad. **❞**

The President gave him a look and said, "I knew it wasn't in Africa."

Secretary Vance looked over his very small glasses and said in an Ivy League tone, "Mr. President, I believe that was in the providence or province of community made up of primitive aborigines. They speak a dialect somewhat different from other villages. They have been around for hundreds of years."

The President looked at him and said, "That's no better than his answer."

Haywood liked that. He knew it was coming and just smiled.

PRESIDENT JOHNSON AND THE 21 GUN SALUTE

Haywood took the President to an event where he was going to receive some type of an award. All the troops were standing at attention, and Haywood taxied Air Force One right up to them. The President walked out the door of the plane and stood on the last step.

"We taxied pretty close. He was standing on that step and when the first cannon went off, it was very loud. The President jumped about two feet in the air right off that step. He thought somebody was shooting at him with a cannon. It's funny now, but it wasn't funny then. He was some kind of mad."

TAKING THE JET-STAR TO ST. LOUIS – A SECRET . . . UNTIL NOW

The St. Louis Cardinals were playing the New York Yankees in the World Series. Stan Musial invited Haywood to attend and sent the Colonel six tickets right behind the St. Louis dugout.

Haywood really wanted to go so he took a few friends in the Jet-Star, landed just outside of St. Louis, and put the plane in a hangar as soon as they got there. They went to the game and were having a great time. The only thing wrong was that Smith never officially asked to take the President's plane to the game.

At the end of the seventh inning, the Colonel called and checked in with Marvin, his boss. He said, "Where are you?"

Haywood paused and said, "Why?"

"We may be going to the Ranch later this afternoon."

"This flag came from the Ranch. I was traveling with the President back there for the last time. So, he actually took it down. He looked at me and asked, 'You want that flag'? 'Yes sir. I do', I said."

Smith said, "Okay" and hung up.

They beat a trail to the hangar, flew back to Washington in time for him to take the President down to the Ranch in Air Force One.

Nobody ever knew about it. Until now.

THE PRESIDENTIAL FLAG

The flag of the president of the United States consists of the presidential coat of arms on a dark blue background. "It flies wherever the President is in residence," Haywood explained. "If the President goes somewhere and stays for even a day, the flag goes with him." The flag is often displayed by the president in official photos, or flown next to the casket of a former President in official funeral processions, and flown on the President's motorcade.

Toward the end of LBJ's term of office he was kind and thoughtful enough to make the rounds and say goodbye to people who had supported him over the course of his presidency.

In a meeting with the military aides on Nov. 22, 1968, he singled out the Colonel for helping hold inter-service rivalries down to a low roar. "Haywood has made decisions when you wouldn't know whether he was in the Air Force or in the Army. He is not in either. That same thing is true of the rest of you."

That was the last Presidential flag that flew over the Ranch. It is now on the Colonel's wall in his den.

"Mr. President, I've got to get back to the Marine Corps."

CHAPTER FOUR

BACK TO THE CORPS

Upon concluding his assignment with President Johnson and upon Richard Nixon's inauguration, our nation was mired in a seemingly endless armed conflict in Southeast Asia. Having never been attacked by the "enemy" to precipitate such a conflict, the US had never actually declared war, and thus, except for those doing the fighting, was never all-in as a nation with the endeavor. That said, Marines exist to fight the nation's battles. Whether declared formally as a war or not, Marines don't get to pick and choose which ones they want to engage in.

THAT'S HELICOPTERS

Haywood thought Vietnam was where he needed to be. However, after President Johnson left office, he wanted him to accompany them back to the Ranch. Mrs. Johnson loved him, too, and wanted Smith to come stay at the Ranch, as well. She privately encouraged Haywood to run for political office. She promised the Johnsons' full support. But Haywood felt like he wasn't doing that much at the Ranch. He was serving at Johnson's convenience.

"I didn't mind doing that as long as I felt like I was being useful. President Johnson sent me back to give President Nixon a military briefing on some verbal agreements Johnson had with other leaders, which went fine." Nixon thanked Haywood and they got to know each other better.

The next time that Smith went back to brief President Nixon, he didn't get to see him. Henry Kissinger said that he didn't need to talk to the President and to

> **"**Thank you, Haywood, for your help during my first months as President, I also appreciate the key role you played in my trip to Memphis.**"**
>
> *Richard Nixon, President*

tell him, instead. So, the Colonel did and that was the last time he went to talk to President Nixon in the Oval Office.

While he was in Washington, he went to the Pentagon to check his jacket (personnel file). Haywood hadn't looked at it in over five years. He immediately noticed a big red sheet that said, *Not to go out of the continental United States for six years.* This was because of his clearance rating and the information he knew. This was going to be a huge roadblock to him serving in Vietnam.

He thought about it for a moment and then just took it out of the file.

He told the President he needed to go to Vietnam. "Mr. President, I've got to get back to the Marine Corps." Two weeks later, he was at Marine Corps Headquarters to be reassigned.

The General said, "Colonel, you haven't been to Vietnam."

"I know. I need to go."

He said, "Well you don't have to go. But I'll send you if you want to go."

"I want to go."

Expecting to lead an attack group of fighters, Smith went to get requalified in the A-4 Skyhawk, a light, single-engine, carrier-capable attack jet used heavily in Vietnam by the Navy and Marines. Requalification would take a month.

But, when he got there, the General said, "I'm glad you're over here, Colonel. I need help in Mag-16."

"General, that's helicopters." Like he didn't know.

He said, "I know. But I know you've flown helicopters and that's where the war is. That's where I need you."

Colonel Smith knew the mission to extract the Marines was dangerous. He just had no idea how dangerous it was going to be . . .

Change of Command of Mag-16.

Marble Mountain.

COMMANDING MAG-16

BRING A BIG CHALKBOARD AND A LOT OF CHALK!

The Colonel took over Mag-16, which included well over a hundred helicopters. As Commanding Officer of the base, he also commanded a large number of army personnel. "It was a huge group with more squadrons than usual. There were about 30 Hueys, 25 Cobras, three 46 Transport Helicopters, and a 56 squadron that could pick up damaged helicopters. The base's air strip, Marble Mountain, was only 15 miles away from Da Nang.

The Colonel was chosen as C.O. for his knowledge and leadership, and his Marines did everything he asked of them. During the American engagement in Vietnam, an estimated two million Vietnamese civilians and 1.4 million soldiers were killed, including 58,220 Americans. To this day, he profoundly regrets that he was not able to bring home all the Marines entrusted to his command.

One day the Commandant came over to visit and saw the Colonel standing at attention in the line and asked, "Haywood, what are you doing here?"

"This is my group, General."

He said, "I didn't know you were the Group Commander. What would you do if you got shot down? There's a lot of information they could get out of you."

"I'd tell them to get a big chalkboard and a lot of chalk because I can't stand pain," the Colonel said.

The General looked at Haywood and laughed. He never said another word to him or to anybody else. Smith stayed and did his tour.

A FIGHT WITH LITTLE EDDIE

There was a door gunner in a 46 aircraft that loved to fly but kept getting in fights. He was certainly not the first or the last Marine who could not hold his temper.

The Sergeant Major said, "Colonel, I have a suggestion for how we can help him control his temper. Let's set up a fight with him and Little Eddie."

Fred Smith on comms in the field.

Fred Smith is a good Marine and an even better friend.

> **"Haywood is a confidant and trusted friend."**

Frederick W. Smith, Founder and Executive Chairman, FedEx

112 MY BEST DAY

Little Eddie only weighed about 150 pounds. But he was a professional boxer. He trained every day. He would run up and down the beach for hours at a time. He was in perfect shape.

So, the next time that Marine got in trouble, Smith had a make-shift ring built. Everybody on the base showed up for the fight. Outweighing Little Eddie by fifty pounds and thinking himself a good fighter, he just smiled. He was going to kill him.

"The bell rang, and then Little Eddie started hitting him everywhere he could be hit, and he hit him a lot," Haywood remembers wryly.

"We never had any more trouble from him."

FRED SMITH IN VIETNAM

While in Vietnam, the Colonel encountered another Memphian, a young Marine Captain also named Smith, Fred Smith. He controlled the military missions and assisted in locating enemy targets. He received high recognition for his service, including a Silver Star, Bronze Star, and two Purple Hearts. He served two tours in Vietnam. That work set him up for success in shipping, as he went on to found Federal Express Corporation (FedEx) after the war.

"Fred was a good Marine in Vietnam. He is as good a friend as I have ever had. He calls often and visits regularly. He is quick to ask about my family. I'm proud of him and always will be."

Fred Smith recalls these things about Vietnam and Haywood Smith:

"My first tour in Vietnam was as a platoon leader and then Company Commander (K Company 3rd Battalion 5th Marine Regiment K/3/5). By the way, K/3/5 was Eugene Sledge's outfit immortalized in his famous book about WWII With the Old Breed."

"My second tour was as a Tactical Air Controller (Airbourne)/Aerial Observer assigned to Marine Observation Squadron 2 (VMO-2) at Marble Mountain airfield near Da Nang."

"Colonel Haywood Smith commanded the Marine Air Group (MAG 36 as I

Me in front of the Hooch with Doug McCauffey, a Blue Angel. The fellow in the middle was an A-4 pilot, who was shot down.

In front of the Hooch, and the concertina wire in the background.

recall) which included helicopters and OV10A Broncos flown by VMO-2. As you note, the Group CO would not be expected to fly the number of missions Haywood did."

"I can assure you going into a "hot LZ" in an assault helicopter like the CH46 was a tough way to make a living."

"Lieutenant Colonel Bill Leftwich from Memphis was killed in one of Haywood's helicopters trying to extricate one of his recon teams. In Memphis, our newly upgraded Leftwich Tennis Center in Audubon Park is named in his honor."

THE HOOCH

Colonel Smith lived in a large hooch at Marble Mountain, right by the ocean. It was big enough to have some officers' meetings there. And because it had a very long bar, he hosted some social occasions there. The hooch was built by the Corps of Engineers. They were great on building bridges and runways, but they weren't great on building hooches. They had no idea what they were doing. Because Marble Mountain housed so many assets, the base was very fortified and protected. As a matter of fact, all the Marine helicopters were there. Barbed or constantine wire, surrounded our living quarters. Military police patrolled constantly. Sentries were in place, surveying the perimeter.

Even so, the Viet Cong were always trying to get through our defenses and destroy our helicopters. With thousands of highly trained Marines stationed there, the VC were also looking for ways to kill them. "If you kill the pilots, you take care of helicopter attacks."

Haywood was the Base Commander and the Group Commander. Even though they generally felt safe, they knew they were still in a very dangerous environment. One day, one of his Lieutenants came up and asked, "Colonel, are you getting a haircut anytime soon?"

"Why?" I asked.

"We got your barber."

"What do you mean?"

> **“**Colonel Smith was my pilot and comrade.**”**
>
> *Dwight Eisenhower, President, General, Supreme Allied Commander*

"He was coming under the concertina barbwire and we shot him."

"My barber?"

"Yes sir." He paused for a minute and reflected. "He could have cut your throat anytime he wanted."

SAVED BY THE CORPS OF ENGINEERS

"One night, I was asleep in my hooch. Now I'm a very sound sleeper. You have to be a sound sleeper to get a good night's sleep in the middle of an active war zone. As a matter of fact, if I had an early launch, I asked a Lieutenant to come wake me up."

"The Corps of Engineers didn't know as much about building a hooch as they did about larger projects. Case in point: they put my door on backwards."

"As usual, I was sound asleep, but something woke me up. It was the rattling of that door. Someone was trying to get in but didn't know the door closed instead of opened. That made such a racket I was immediately awake and alert, and yelled, '*Who's there?*'"

"Then I heard the shuffling of feet. I jumped up, grabbed my gun and ran to that door, No one was there. I thought, "He went out the front door."

"So I ran out the front door, but didn't see him, so I shouted to the officers in their hooches. They came running out. When they heard what happened, they called my Shore Patrol. They went in the hooch and discovered he had come in a window and then left through the window. They also determined he exited under the barbed wire, which was the same way he came in."

"I thought about that and figured the Corps of Engineers saved my life. If that door hadn't been put on backwards, he would have killed me. My thought was, I guess the Lord wasn't ready for me to go yet. He had something for me to do. I've thought about what that was. A few times since then, I've thought I found the Lord's purpose for me. But I'm still here. I haven't got it done. Maybe if I don't find what it is, I'll live forever."

"I guess the Lord wasn't ready for me to go yet. He had something for me to do."

MORTAR ATTACK

The Colonel flew over two hundred missions himself during Vietnam. Every one was dangerous. But he felt strongly that he should show his Marines that he wasn't asking them to do anything he wasn't prepared to do. It was on one of those missions to join a strike in Cambodia, when he understood they were not supposed to be there.

They were to set down in a small landing zone and prepare for a strike early the next morning. They were flying Cobras and 46s which had carried the troops in. Cobra squadron Commander, Harry Sexton, and Haywood were sitting around a campfire. Suddenly, they heard a loud whooshing and thumping noise.

Harry said, "What was that?"

"I don't know. It must be outgoing."

Harry said, "We don't have any outgoing."

They both knew that was not good.

Harry jumped up and said, "Let's go!"

"Wait a minute!" Haywood said.

But Harry didn't wait. The sound turned out to be mortars the Viet Cong were firing at the Colonel's helicopters. And they were close. He piloted the Cobra and got them out. Running on fumes, he arrived back on base, having accomplished the mission.

"Harry represented the kind of Marine pilots I worked with. They were brave and they were very good pilots. He risked his life that day to save a lot of other lives, like mine. Those actions happened on a regular basis. Harry was able to return to base. Many brave pilots didn't."

WHAT NOT TO FORGET

Another time, the Colonel was in a 46 that was transporting some troops on a mission. He had an automatic weapon that provided good ground cover. His crew unloaded the troops and had just taken off. The pilot said, "They've hit

The Seaboard DC-8 landing accidentally on our runway at Marble Mountain.

The airline crew were waiting to see if the pilot could manage the take-off.

120 MY BEST DAY

our oil line." Haywood looked out. Oil was spraying everywhere, so they had to land.

They set the aircraft down in a field of tall elephant grass. This put Haywood in an even more dangerous situation. The Colonel, his accompanying Sergeant Major and the pilot jumped out of the helicopter into the long grass and assumed a position to wait for another helicopter to come pick them up. The Sergeant Major looked over at Smith's weapon and said, "Colonel what are you going to do with that?"

He looked down and realized that he had run out of the helicopter without his clip! The Sergeant Major never let him forget about it. For years, he would send him a Christmas card and say, "I've still got your clip."

THE JET THAT LANDED AT MARBLE MOUNTAIN BY MISTAKE

Marble Mountain was about three and a half miles from Da Nang's airport. Da Nang had an 8,000-foot runway. It was used for larger aircraft that transported the troops. Much of the time, civilian airlines were used to bring the troops in and to take them away.

One day when visibility was low, a large civilian aircraft, Seaboard DC-8, landed at Marble Mountain by mistake. The pilot barely got the plane stopped before he would have run out of pavement.

"The good news was that there were eight good looking flight attendants aboard. That was the plus side, and it probably got him an extra day on the base. The bad news was that the plane was too big to take off on a 3,400-foot runway."

The pilot came in and asked the Colonel what they could do about it.

Haywood said, "Well, I'll tell you what we're going to do. You've got a day and a half to get it out of here or I'm going to blow it up. I have to have my airstrip back. I can't have your plane stopping the war because you screwed up."

The pilot said, "What do you mean?"

Smith responded, "I mean I'm going to blow it up!"

> **The Colonel always said: There were no black or white Marines. They were all green.**

With Col. Skinny Lamar and our XOs.

122 MY BEST DAY

He looked at the commercial pilot for a minute, then said, "Maybe you haven't noticed, but you just landed on a military base that's in the most dangerous spot in the world. On top of that, you're blocking my runway."

The pilot said, "You can't do that!"

"Wait until tomorrow," the Colonel said.

The captain started calling the airline. The higher ups. The airline said the Marines couldn't blow it up. Since Haywood didn't report to an airline and since the Marble Mountain runway was his lifeline, he didn't much care what an airline V.P. said.

When the airline called the Marine Corps Base at Quantico, they were told, "If Colonel Smith said he was going to blow it up, get ready. He's going to blow it up!"

To his credit, the captain said he was going to try to fly it off the runway.

So, the pilot stripped the plane. He took out the seats and everything else that could be removed. He left just enough fuel to make the short hop to Da Nang.

When he took off, everybody was standing by the runway to see if he made it, including the Colonel.

"I didn't think he was going to make it, but at least we weren't going to have to get it off the runway. He was heading for the ocean."

The pilot got it off the runway and made the trip to Da Nang. "We were happy about that, but sad that meant the flight attendants would be leaving soon."

SECRET MISSION

They were preparing for an assault, right outside of Vietnam, so Colonel Smith went back to Cambodia on a secret mission.

In his military experience, the Cambodian allies who fought alongside were the fiercest fighters the Colonel had ever seen. He would gladly stand beside them in battle.

A REVERSAL IN THE WAY THE WAR WAS VIEWED

At one time, the Vietnam war was not popular. It was a different kind of war. In the second World War, a soldier was only in combat for a little more than a month at a time. In Vietnam, ground Marines were in the war EVERY day for several months at a time. "I recently read that although only two million soldiers actually went to Vietnam, over seven million claim to have served. I guess the attitude has changed.

One night, as it was getting dark and Haywood was sitting by the fire. The Cambodian Commanding Officer sat down and said, "Colonel, you want to sleep in my tent?"

Smith said that he might lay down awhile and thanked him. After a bit, the Commander came into the tent, yelling, "Alice!"

The Colonel knew there was not a woman in the tent, but the Commander kept repeating her name. Haywood asked, "Who are you calling? I've told you there's no woman in here!"

The Commander was looking under Haywood's bed and said, "I've got a pet python in here somewhere."

"I got my gear and decided to sleep out by the fire."

STORY OF A CORPORAL'S VALOR

Corporal Raymond Michael Clausen, Jr. was one of the Marines that Smith nominated for the Medal of Honor, but he didn't start out in high honors. As a Marine who kept getting into fights on base, Corporal Clausen was brought to Haywood because his C.O. had done all he could for him and was about to give up. He wanted Haywood to see if he agreed.

So, the Corporal came in, the Colonel said, "Clausen, we don't need you. You're not going to able to fly anymore."

That got his attention. "I'll do anything if you'll let me keep flying."

Haywood stared at him for a long time and said, "Alright, then quit your behavior and act like a Marine. We have to fight enough out there without having you fight another Marine all the time. Next time I hear that you have a fight, you'll never fly again under my command."

He promised he would change, and Smith knew he could. "And he did, he became a real Marine."

Two weeks later, Corporal Clausen was the crew chief for the CH-46 on a mission. These helicopters inserted Marines into tricky situations. He was a

" That's where the war is. That's where I need you. "

I often flew the Cobra helicopter. Equipped with missiles, machine guns, and bombs, the Cobras helped save thousands of Marines when they had to be evacuated.

shooter or door gunner. They were trying to cut off a battalion of the V.C., and the Marines ran into a mine field. The survivors stood where they were. The Squadron Commander said he was going in to bring out some of the wounded. Most were already dead. Clausen heroically stuck his bayonet in the ground to make sure the helicopter wasn't about to land on a mine.

The Medic jumped out and retrieved a wounded Marine. He went back for another, stepped on a mine and blew up. Then Clausen ran out and picked one up. Then another. Then another. Then another. Then one more. Four of the five lived.

He received the Medal of Honor at Haywood's recommendation. "That's the highest honor they could give."

Years later, when Smith was stationed in New Orleans as the Commanding Officer of six states, The Sergeant Major came in his office and asked the Colonel, "Do you know anybody named Clausen?"

"Yeah, why?"

"He's out here to see you."

He was a civilian but wanted to come by and say hello and to thank Haywood for being his Colonel and giving him a second chance in Vietnam. He thanked him for recommending him for the Medal of Honor. Subsequently, he said, he never had to buy a drink, as he wore his medal proudly.

FLYING EVERY KIND OF HELICOPTER IN VIETNAM

In the more than two hundred missions the Colonel flew in Vietnam, he qualified and flew all types of helicopters: Cobras, the 46s, 53s and the Hueys. "That's What the C.O. does."

Of all the helicopters, his favorite to fly was the Cobra. It held a crew of two and had formidable firepower. The pilot in the front operated the cannons and the machine guns. The pilot in the back piloted the aircraft and operated the rockets on each side. It was fast, could fly at low altitudes, and did a lot more damage than any other helicopter. Better still was the fact that the V.C. did not have any helicopters.

Sometimes if they were going to do an insert, using a lot of 46s with a whole Company of men, they wanted to make sure the V.C. had not laid a trap with troops all around. That was when the Cobras would swoop in and shoot the entire area to ensure that it was safe. The hardest missions, though, were recons and extracts, because they had to be stationary as they were evacuating, which made them even more susceptible to being shot down.

Of the almost 12,000 helicopters used in Vietnam, almost half were shot down. The Colonel learned quickly to put a thick, heavy metal plate under his seat cushion as "life insurance." He never went on a mission without getting a few new holes in whatever helicopter he was flying. The V.C. started shooting at them as soon as they got in the air. They could hear them land and take off.

"Everybody on the ground took a shot at us and we were often an easy target. Our helicopters usually flew under 1500 feet. Flying that low, we were a target for every V.C. with a gun in the jungle."

Haywood received a medal every time the helicopter he was piloting was hit with enemy fire.

"I got so many, I just put them in a drawer."

Haywood thought quite often that these medals were not appropriate. When he mentioned this to the General, he was sternly informed that, "Any time you are being shot at, you are in harm's way. Furthermore, it was only a matter of time before one of those rounds does critical damage to the helicopter or the pilot."

A FIRM MATTRESS

As with his helicopter seat, he put a thick piece of metal under his mattress at the hooch. So, instead of heading for the bunker when the alarm sounded for incoming, we would just roll over, take his pillow and get under the bed. "Maybe I was tired. Or lazy. Or stubborn. Besides, no matter what happened, it never lasted too long."

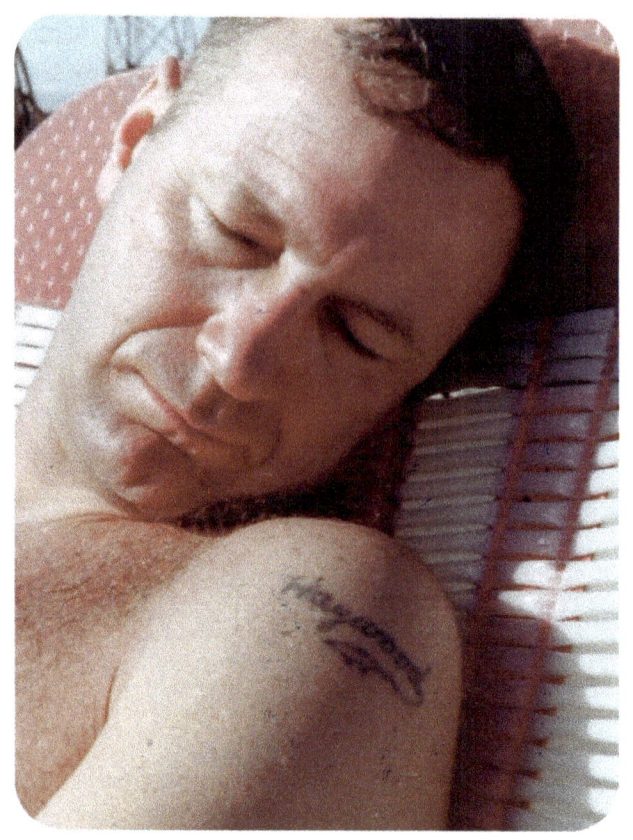

THE COLONEL'S PACKIN'

The Colonel wore a sidearm at all times. He used a pistol that was given to him when he left the White House. It was a Smith and Wesson. He also carried a sawed off automatic carbine.

130 MY BEST DAY

NOT THE PRESIDENT

An observation from fellow Marine, Capt. John Darracott, Adjutant of MAG-16:

"Colonel Haywood Smith, the Group Commander, prior to his MAG-16 tour had served for four-plus years as Military Aide to President Johnson. For some reason, the Colonel thought his White House days carried over to Vietnam with him. When President Johnson wanted something done, he would just tell Col. Smith what it was and when he wanted it. Col. Smith made the phone calls, saying the President wants etc. etc. and magic would happen. The President's wishes happened."

"One day while serving as the Colonel's Adjutant, he called out from his office and asked me to get him the motion picture *Patton* for his hooch tonight. Being a devoted Adjutant I called every Special Services Officer I knew, but found *Patton* was not even in-country. Frustrated after an afternoon on the phone trying to satisfy the Colonel's desires, I had to go tell him the film was not in-country."

"'Darracott', he said, 'when I was at the President's ranch in Texas, and he wanted to see a film, I would call Hollywood and they would fly it to the Ranch.' Becoming totally unglued and very upset because I could not perform, I blurted out: 'That's great Colonel, but this ain't the Ranch and you are not the President.'"

"I realized what I had said - dead silence - waiting for the wrath of Haywood to fall on my head or even orders to the grunts to be effective immediately - but the Colonel came out of his office laughing and said, 'Darracott, you're OK. Let's go to the club and get a beer.' I was born again with those words!"

"It was a pleasure and honor working for a man of his talents."

SOMETIMES, THE BEST ANTIDOTE IS PLAY

As described in the book, *Shackleton*, and movie by the same title, the Antarctic explorer, Sir Ernest Shackleton who, when in 1914 his mission went wrong, found himself caught with his men in the Antarctic ice pack with no hope of rescue. He deliberately built some frivolity - or play time - into their routine to

Me and the officers of Mag-16.

Lew Walt, a 4-star General and Assistant Commandant of the Marine Corps made a visit to Mag-16 in Viet Naam.

keep them from losing all hope, not to mention their senses.

Like Shackleton, Colonel Smith unflinchingly expected a lot from his troops but he also believed that, under the stress of combat, they needed regular opportunities to forget about business and blow off a little steam. Here they were, in the middle of a terrible war, with those they loved being injured or killed. They were in the middle of hell, you might say. So, the Colonel created all kinds of diversionary activities.

In addition to his own accounts, there are reports to suggest and confirm that Col. Smith went to great lengths and exercised considerable ingenuity in creating those opportunities, often in the form of pranks occurring at the expense of his peers and their units.

HELOS VS. JETS ROUND 1

An example of these antics took place when he took his entire staff of 46 Commanders to Chu Li, about a hundred miles away. There was a fighter pilot group there, and they had invited them to come for "Happy Hour." The fighter pilots began to give his staff a hard time. As jet pilots, they thought they were smarter and superior to the helicopter pilots.

"They didn't realize that all of our helicopter pilots had been fighter pilots at one time. The Marines put some of the best fighter pilots in the helicopters and changed the whole face of the helicopter operation. The skill, agility, and flight experience of those pilots took the capability of our company to an unbelievable level."

Haywood had the jeep that belonged to the Colonel of that group picked up by one of his helicopters and placed on the roof of a building. Since the fighter pilot base did not have a helicopter, they knew he couldn't get it down. He was not very happy.

The General would hear about what the Colonel did and would chew him out good. Then he would laugh and say he wished he could have been there. He understood. One time he said, "I don't know how you come up with these ideas, Haywood. But keep them coming."

Planning the get-even with the fixed wing pilots.

HELOS VS. JETS ROUND 2

As the pranks heated up between the helo and jet pilots, it was time to take it to the next level, especially with the jet pilots thinking they were so much better! They constantly made fun of the helo pilots, even though most of them, like the Colonel, flew jets first.

Haywood invited the Group Commander and all of the Squadron Commanders, to his hooch to play volleyball, swim in the ocean and eat some steaks. The Colonel sent a helicopter to pick them up. It was getting dark and the Group Commander, who was also a Colonel, reminded him that they had to be back before dark.

They all got in a 46 and Smith was the pilot. About halfway back, he announced that they were having some engine trouble and put the 46 down in a rice field. It was about a foot and a half deep in water.

He said, "You're all going to have to get out. There's another 46 on its way to pick you up."

The 46 came, but set down about a hundred yards away, so they had to tromp through deep mud to get to it. Just as they were about to get in, it took off and so did Haywood. They had an eight mile hike to get back to their base.

That was not all they did, though. Smith had his officers take off their identification to make them look like they were enlisted. They went over to the Group Commander's hooch, climbed up on the roof and painted a large bullseye! In the process, they broke a window or two, objects that were hard to replace.

The Group Commander was not happy!

The next day at about five a.m. two F-4s came over Haywood's hooch at about twenty feet and hit their afterburners. BOOM!

That revenge happened for several days.

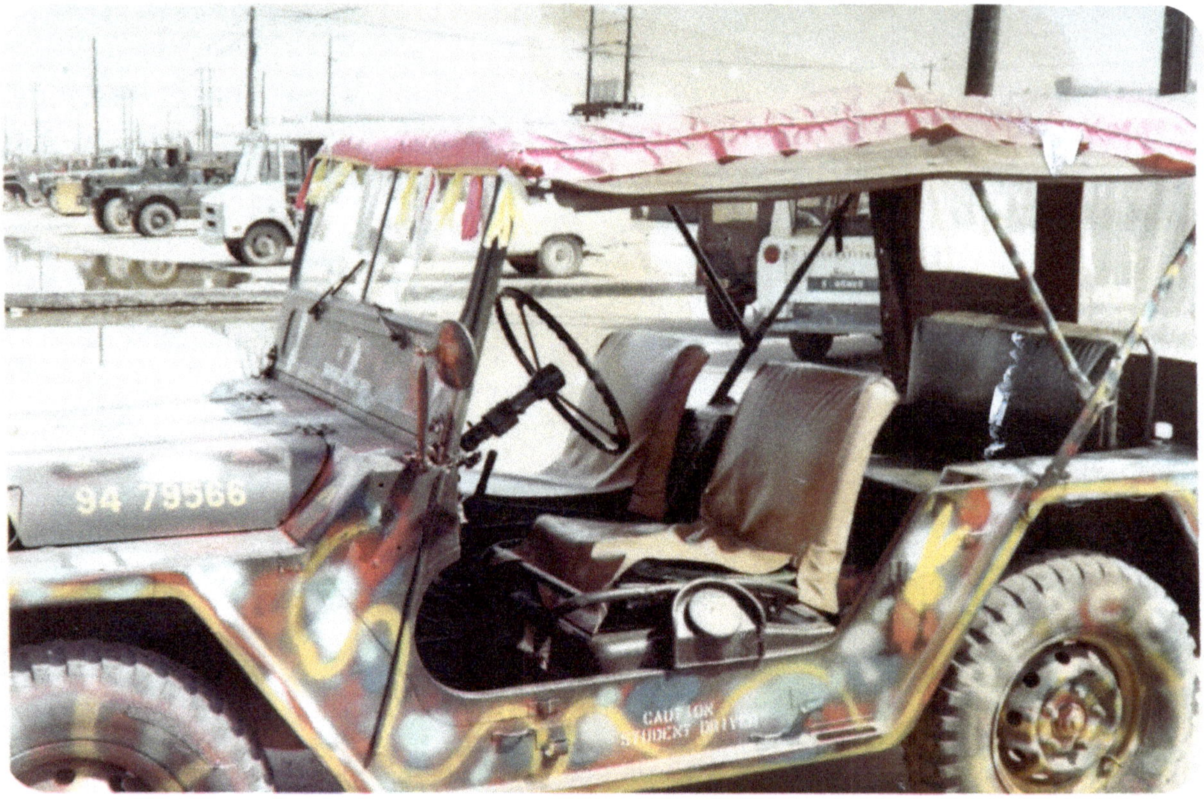
94 79566
CAUTION
STUDENT DRIVER

MAC
16
CD
11
4 79566

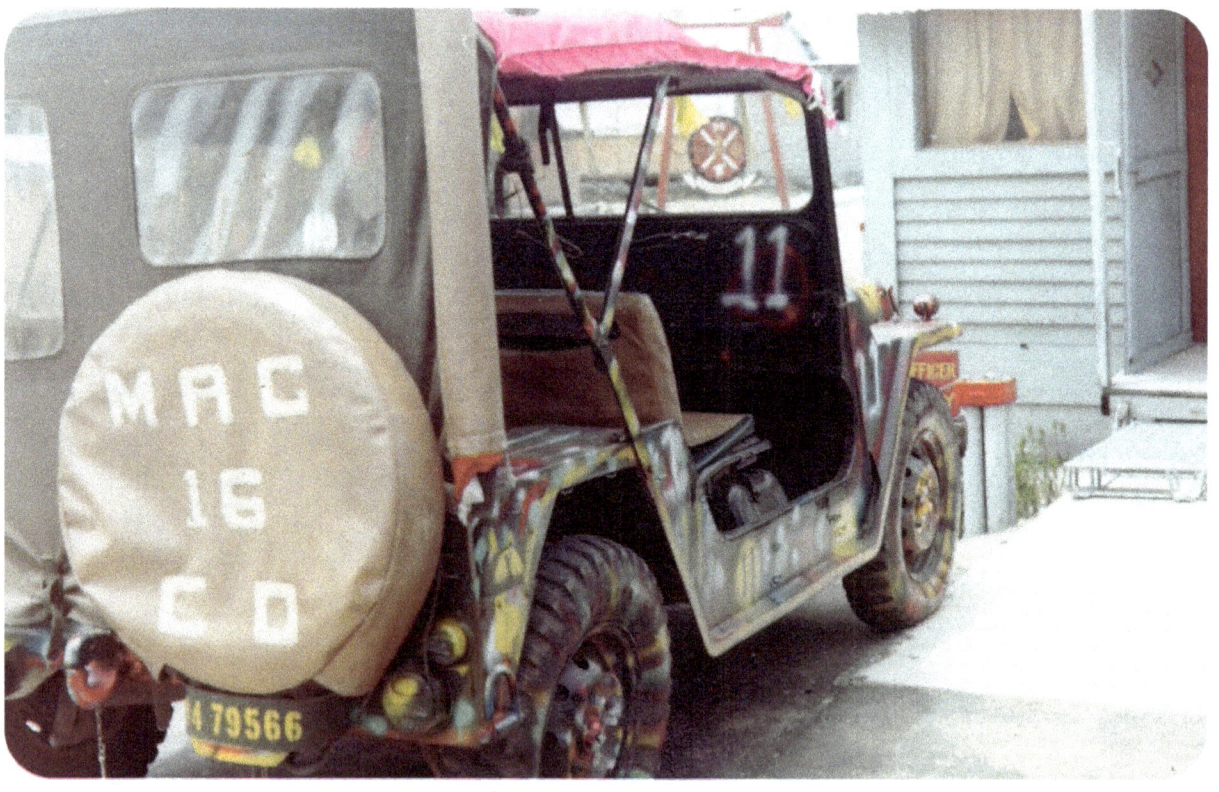

JET PILOTS FIGHT BACK

To retaliate for marooning his group staff in that rice field, the MAG-11 commander decided on a plan to embarrass Smith in front of his own people.

He knew that Haywood would drive over from Marble Mountain and park in the wing headquarters compound. While he was in a meeting, they drained most of the fuel from the tank of his Jeep, and they raised the ante on the prank by painting the vehicle in a dozen different and bizarre colors.

They had assumed that Haywood would get in his Jeep and head back to Marble Mountain, but would run out of fuel on the middle of the bridge and have to call Mag-11 for a tow.

But that is not what happened. Instead, Haywood emerged from wing headquarters, took one look at this jeep and went back inside and picked up a telephone. He called over to one of his CH-53 squadrons, which dutifully sent a plane to the wing helipad. Within minutes, he and his jeep were safely back at Marble Mountain without anyone of note having seen it.

Even though the Mag-11 prank had very low impact, the paint really bothered Haywood, so he called his raiders into conference and started working on a plan for revenge.

HELOS GET THE LAST WORD

The Mag-11 Commander, Colonel Pomerenck also had a hooch that was built by the Corps. While it wasn't as nice as Haywoods, he was pretty proud of it.

One day when the MAG-11 staff was away, Smith sent in ten or twelve lieutenants dressed in grungy coveralls, each carrying a paint bucket and brush, and a couple of ladders between them. Within twenty minutes, they had painted the Group Commander's house in the same horrible color scheme as they had used on his Jeep.

Colonel Pommerenck was pretty upset about it all, especially the big bull's-eye painted on the roof.

I did have a pretty good paint crew.

LUMINOUS SIX

Haywood's Call Sign was Luminous Six. Everyone knew his call sign.

One time the Colonel radioed a couple of helos, "You're flying a little low, arent' you?"

"Who in the hell is this?" one of the pilots demanded.

"This is Luminous Six."

"Whoo. Yes sir."

For most of 1970, the helicopter air group (MAG-16) was led by Col. Smith whom we used to see on television a lot when he was President Lyndon Johnson's aide. Col. Smith knew there was a difference between the helicopter community and the jet community, because of the selection priorities in the Naval Air Training Command.

Col. Smith and some of his helicopter pilot henchmen paid a courtesy call on the F-4 Phantom pilots of MAG-13. Ostensibly, the visit was a social one in which representatives of the helicopter community were to join with the fighter pilots at Chu Lai during their Friday afternoon happy hour. But there wouldn't be any story to tell if Haywood had stuck to the script.

Some of the helicopter pilots had more pressing chores to attend to and remained with the helicopter under the guise of being designated drivers - backup pilots for the actual crew. They remained with the helicopter until everyone was out of sight.

Later, this raiding party "borrowed" a vehicle on their own, under pretenses of making a run to the mess hall. When a decent interval of time had elapsed, they too, headed for the Officers' club, stopping along the way only to replace a sign.

Borrowing liberally from the bravado of the Navy's replacement air group at NAS Miramar in southern California, MAG-13 had erected a self-serving sign at the entrance to their living area welcoming all to "Fighter Town." In an incredibly short period of time, indicating that the raiding party had practiced a lot, the sign was replaced by one identical in color and format. The only difference was that the new sign, in traditional Marine Corps scarlet and gold, welcomed a visitor to a "different" kind of town.

The new sign, ten by fifteen feet, with 12 inch lettering, was not discovered until two days later, so splendid was the artwork. Haywood Smith not only had balls, he also had a great paint shop. But that clever coup was an afterthought, definitely not the highlight of the visit. Nor was the diversionary tactic of "inciting to riot" in the officers' club of great

importance when Haywood stood at the bar and slandered the entire air group, using a hand-held bullhorn to ensure that even the noisy lieutenants in the back were properly insulted.

All the aircraft at Chu Lai were being used as bombers, the F-4s as well as the A-4 Skyhawks, and it galled Haywood that the F-4 pilots would still call themselves fighter pilots. He announced grandly – a skill he had learned from LBJ - that he wanted to buy a drink for every fighter pilot in the club. The cheering response to this, predictably, was boisterous, and when it subsided, he slapped a one-dollar bill on the bar, and added, "And I expect my change!"

As planned, that got everyone's attention. The screaming and yelling and claims and counterclaims kept everyone busy long enough for the highly skilled terrorists to accomplish their mission. Outside in the parking lot, the raiding party quietly stole the Group Commander's jeep while the helicopter pilots warmed up the CH-53 just as night descended. When the sun came up the next morning, long after the helicopter pilots had departed for home, the MAG-13 Group Commander finally found his jeep - on top of a hangar. He had to get the Army to retrieve it for him - and they dropped it.

I don't recall that there was any animosity between the jet group ad the helicopter group. I think the feuding arose simply because Haywood Smith was bored, and these were the only two air groups in the immediate area.

(From Ground Attack Vietnam: The Marines who Controlled the Skies, J.M. Moriarty, Ballentine Books)

> **"I don't know how you come up with these ideas, Haywood. But keep them coming."**

A TIGHT SPOT

There was a safe beach on the ocean where the Marines could go swimming. It was about an hour's drive from Marble Mountain. Fifteen or so Marines would jump in a truck and take off down a road that passed through a small village. On one of these trips the group was involved in an unfortunate accident that claimed the life of a young local boy.

They called the Colonel, and he told the Sergeant Major, "We've got to go over there."

There were many Viet Cong in the village. As they pulled up to the accident scene, the Sergeant Major said, "This is not good, Colonel. Maybe we ought to go back."

He said, "I'm not going anywhere." So, he found the village chief and an interpreter and said, "This is a terrible accident and I'm sorry. What can I do?"

The chief said he wanted money, so Haywood asked, "Okay, how much?"

He said, "Money, money!"

Haywood returned quickly to the base, to find the General. He hurriedly said, "General, I really don't have time to explain this mess to you, but I need about $2,000."

"What for?"

Smith emphasized, "I don't have time to explain, but I need it right away." The General gave him the money.

He quickly returned to the chief and gave him the money. About that time, a helicopter landed. It was a Vietnamese General. He knew Haywood.

He said, "I heard you were having a problem."

The Colonel told him what was going on. The General asked, "Can I talk to him?" Haywood knew he could continue the conversation without an interpreter and said he could.

The chief said he wanted more money. At that time, the average Vietnamese

“Even the officers feared him. He was there to protect me. He would have died for me.”

person wasn't making much more than $100 a year, and they had just handed over $2,000. While Smith did not understand what they were saying, he could tell the discussion was escalating. Suddenly, the General pulled out a pearl-handled 45 and shot the chief, knocking him back at least ten feet.

Knowing things might get even more heated, the Colonel asked who was the next in charge. A man approached Haywood, who pointed to the sky. Circling above were two Cobras and two Hueys. He said, "If anything happens to my Marines, I'm going to kill all of you."

The Viet Cong had already punctured the truck tires, so Smith ordered, "Drive on the rims. Just get out of here!" They left with sparks flying. With a helicopter escort, they made it back to Marble Mountain safely.

THE SERGEANT MAJOR'S UNIQUE JUSTICE SYSTEM

The Colonel was coming back from a hop to his hooch one night and somebody shot a flare right across the hood of his jeep. He had to drive quickly through the smoke.

He later told the Sergeant Major about it and said he needed to discourage this behavior.

Sergeant Major responded, "Yes sir."

Two or three days later, he said, "Colonel, would you come with me, please?"

"Sure. Where are we going?"

"To my hooch."

They walked into his quarters, and he said, "You know that Marine that shot that flare at your jeep?"

"Yeah, did you ever find who did it?"

He said, "Yeah." He walked over to his locker and opened it. A young, terrified Marine was cowering inside his locker.

The Sergeant Major took care of his Colonel. "Even the officers feared him. He was there to protect me. He would have died for me."

THE NURSES COME TO MARBLE MOUNTAIN

When a Marine was wounded, it was necessary to medivac him out to a hospital or a hospital ship, whichever was closest. On one flight transporting wounded Marines to a hospital ship, Haywood was helping unload the injured, when one of the doctors recognized him as the Commanding Officer of Marble Mountain and alerted the Commanding Officer of the ship that Haywood was aboard.

The C.O. greeted Haywood and observed, "Colonel, you looked a little whipped." He admitted that he was. He said that he had a little medicine in his cabin. Smith followed him back to his quarters and was administered a shot, a shot of Jack Daniels, that is.

They talked about the tremendous workload of the ship's medical staff and the stress they were under. All of their patients had suffered terrible injuries. Many were left in life threatening conditions and, of course, ultimately, many did not survive.

The ship's C.O. said, "These nurses work hard. I hate that they have no place to go to take their mind off things."

Smith thought about that for a second and said, "You know, I've got a really nice beach. Would you like for me to come by sometime and pick up some of your nurses?"

He said, "Boy, that would be a great thing."

The Colonel took his number and said he would call with arrangements. The following day, he telephoned that next Sunday would be a good time.

The C.O. asked, "How many can I send?"

Haywood answered, "Oh, about 20."

So, they transported twenty nurses to Marble Mountain and boy, these girls were having a great time. Just getting off the ship was a great treat for them. They took a tour of the base and if anyone had forgotten what females looked like, they were well reminded. Someone mixed up some cocktails and the nurses were drinking, laughing, and playing volleyball. One of them said it was the first time she had laughed in ages.

Flying the 46 to evacuate recon from enemy territory.

148 MY BEST DAY

"I knew this getaway from what they saw every day was something they desperately needed."

It got to be pretty late and the Commander on the ship called and asked, "Where are my nurses?"

"He didn't sound very happy. So I improvised and yelled, I can't talk to you right now! We're under attack! I'll bring them back as soon as I can. Bye!"

The next call was from the General. He said, "Haywood, what is going on over there?"

When Smith caught him up, he said, "Why didn't you invite me?"

That was the last time they saw the nurses on the beach. Still, at least for one day, they got to slow the war down a little bit.

THE BUGLE ROSS PEROT COULDN'T BUY

Haywood's friend, Lt. Colonel Bill Leftwich, was the Aide to the Secretary of the Navy when Smith was aide to the President. They also fought in Vietnam together. Leftwich had so many medals for being shot at, he couldn't get any more, Haywood recalled. "He was maybe the best Marine I ever met."

Bill was the Commanding Officer of Recon, the best command in the Marine Corps. Some of his marines had been inserted way back behind the V.C.. They were placed there to obtain intelligence on the strength and movement of the enemy. They were very good at what they did, but every now and then, they were spotted. And if they didn't extract them in a hurry, they would be captured or killed.

Recon was always ready for the emergency. There was a 46 helicopter and two Cobras for support. The Commanding Officer is not supposed to go, but Bill went anyway, which was not unusual. He was on the 46, lowering "the string" for the guys on the ground. They had all attached themselves to the line, but as they were under heavy fire, the helo crashed into a mountain. All were killed.

The Colonel still tries not to think about that too much.

Smith was chosen to make the arrangements for Leftwich's funeral. Texas

A young Lt. Colonel Bill Leftwich, the best Marine I ever met.

billionaire Ross Perot was in attendance. It was a beautiful military service. They ended with Taps played on a lone bugle. Ross came to Haywood after the service and said, "I want to buy that bugle."

Smith said, "I'm sorry Mr. Perot. You don't have enough money to buy that bugle."

He said, "I wanted it for Mattie, his mother."

The Colonel said, "Then I'll give it to you."

REFLECTING ON TRAUMA AND LOSS

Colonel Smith can genuinely understand how some soldiers never get over their experiences in the war. Things happen in combat that humans seem incapable of. As he said, "It didn't seem possible to me that such inhuman things were done." Haywood occasionally has terrible memories creep up but for the most part; he has made peace with them.

Still, he often remembers the many wonderful Marines, Soldiers, Sailors, and Airmen who died in Vietnam.

During the Kennedy administration, Defense Secretary, Robert McNamara, presided over a significant part of the United States' involvement in the war. McNamara later wrote a book, in which he confessed that he had been wrong about some of his decisions during the Vietnam War. Haywood concurs, and yet, to this day, regrets that he was unable to return all the Marines entrusted to his leadership home.

VISITING FAMILY OF FALLEN SOLDIERS

When he left Vietnam, the Colonel visited those families of the Marines he lost. Many of those visits, however tough, would also be good visits. Looking for peace of mind and closure, the parents of a Marine wanted to know all about where he was and what he did.

Other visits were humbling. "Once, a mother of a small child, who was the wife of the fallen Marine, wouldn't even let me in the door."

> **"It further reinforced my belief that you and I need to make the most of each day."**

Presenting Jennings with a long overdue combat medal.

In July 2018, several years after his own retirement, Col. Smith displayed the devotion that Marines have to one another when he volunteered to officiate at the presentation of a long overdue combat medal to a fellow airman, Lt. Col. John (Jack) Jennings, who had displayed valor in the skies over Laos in April, 1966.

"As I think back to my time in Vietnam, I have many emotions. Pride in a group of Marines who did what they were asked, regardless of the danger. Joy in the times that I was able to distract their minds enough to enjoy a volleyball game or a swim at the beach or some harmless pranks. Sad that I wasn't able to bring them all home."

"As I worked on this book, I began to have Post Traumatic Stress over 50 years after Vietnam. I've fallen out of bed. I've had horrible dreams. I'm told that these will go away soon. I hope so."

"My life was changed during those years. It further reinforced my belief that you and I need to make the most of each day. Wherever we are, whatever our assignment in life is, and whatever our opportunities are."

> "It doesn't matter what you have. It matters what you have inside."

The day I took command of the Marines at Millington, TN, which brought me back home to Memphis.

CHAPTER 5

LIFE AFTER NAM

SPAGHETTI FOR SUPPER

As Jack Jennings remembers, "Haywood and I, and our wives were invited to Earl Lovell's place one night to eat dinner. So, the wives were in the kitchen making spaghetti with meatballs. Meanwhile, we, the three husbands, were still at happy hour with the squadron."

"We were supposed to eat at 8:00. Well, we showed up about 10:30. We were still in uniform. His (Lovell's) wife was fit to be tied, and our wives weren't very happy either. We sat down at the table and announced that we were ready to eat."

"His wife told us that dinner had already been served. It had come and gone. We were out of luck. Earl slammed his hand on the table and said, 'Alma, this is my castle and I'm the king. Now you go get that spaghetti. I'm ready to be served."

Alma walked into the kitchen, picked up the big pot of spaghetti, came out and turned it over Earl's head and said, "There you are, King. Here's your crown."

CAN'T STAND THE HEAT?

On a particularly hot day, Earl Lovell and Haywood went to play golf. "I had a new Pontiac. It was beautiful. Earl needed a ride home, so he hopped in. He said, 'Haywood it is really hot in here'."

The Colonel said, "Well shut the door and I'll turn on the air conditioner."

> **"What a great time we had at the World Series. I'm glad you enjoyed my restaurant. Go Cardinals!"**
>
> *Stan Musial, professional baseball player*

Welcome Aboard! Colonel Haywood Smith you've inherited a great tradition here in Arkansas. Semper Fidelis Sept. 8, 1972 Bob Riley

Lovell shut the door and Haywood pushed the button. After a couple of minutes, he said, "Haywood, when is the air conditioner coming on?"

"He didn't realize that I had the heat on. After another half a mile, he said, 'Pull over, pull over.'"

"I did and he just fell out of that car. He was lying on the ground, breathing heavy. I guess he thought he was having a stroke."

He did not think it was very funny.

CATS

One night, outside the Smith's base house in Millington, they heard a cat yelling. The next day, the kids started playing with it. Then the cat started bringing little presents up to the doorstep, like mice she caught in the field.

The kids really got to be fond of the cat and named her Joan of Ark. They all called her Joanie. Since she was a well-behaved cat, they let her in the house. She took up residence in Haywood's closet, and a few days later they found that she had six kittens. While they were pretty little kittens, the Smiths could not keep seven cats in their house. But what could they do? Haywood came up with a plan.

So, the first time he went to the Officers Club, he took three of those kittens with him. They were in a box. He put it up on the counter. Everybody came around and said, "What have you got, Colonel?"

He said, "Well, I wanted you to see my kittens. They are a breed from Russia."

"From Russia?" a Lieutenant asked.

"Yeah, I don't think there are any in our country quite like these."

Another Lieutenant asked, "What are you going to do with them?"

"I haven't decided yet."

A Captain said, "Well, I'd like to have one."

Another Captain came up and asked what was going on. He asked for a kitten.

Scenes of the crash.

The Lieutenants fought over the third one.

He gave all three cats away in less than ten minutes. The other officers were disappointed.

So, Haywood shook his head and said, "Well, I do have some more at home, but I don't know. I kind of wanted to keep them." They begged him to bring them, and he did. He could have given away twenty cats that night.

THE COLONEL'S LOW ALTITUDE JET CRASH

As a test pilot, Smith and his copilot were attempting a takeoff, but he could not get the nose off the pavement. Taking the appropriate course of action, they ejected out of the plane. The other pilot died, and Haywood should have but he landed in a fence that buffered his fall. When the ambulance crew was rushing him to the hospital, he heard one of the attendants say, "This one isn't going to make it."

He spent a few months in the hospital recovering from a broken neck. During that time, he received a number of visits, especially from Marine personnel. The Colonel let everyone know that he didn't think it was quite fair that alcoholic beverages were prohibited in the military hospital.

"The Squadron Commander told the Duty Officer to help me out." Each Friday, the Marines would show up with a half-gallon of rum and coke. His hospital room was on the ground floor and the Marines created a solution to the problem. They put the container of alcohol in a garbage can just below the window. They ran a rubber tube from the alcohol container, through the top of the trash can and into the base of the window. From there, they ran the tube alongside the many tubes beside his bed. It fit right in. Just another IV tube. This contraband tube ran beside his pillow with a mouthpiece that allowed him to take a swig any time he wanted.

The nurses were really upset when they discovered Smith was receiving alcohol from the outside. They began to search everyone who came to visit. "They could not figure out how I could possibly be getting booze from the outside."

There was a Marine down the hall that had been blinded in an accident. His

Rocking in front of our building on base.

nickname was Red because of his red hair. "I could hear him tapping his hands on the hallway wall one day. He walked in and said, 'I'm glad I finally found you. Someone said you had something to drink in here.'"

"I told him to come on in. I told him to come over to my bed and to bend over and I gave him the tube. He took a long pull. He sat down and we talked for a long time. Of course, the longer we talked, the more he was able to drink."

It turned out that Red was a big drinker. Every time he came to visit, which was pretty often, he drank a little more. One day, as he left the room, he was staggering along while patting the wall. Haywood heard a nurse yell, "He's drunk!"

The nurses came in and searched again. The Charge Nurse asked, "How did he get drunk?"

"I told her, 'I don't have any idea. I hope he's okay'."

"They never let Red come back to my room. But they never did discover my alcohol source."

He went home to rehabilitate. "I had weights attached to my neck while I was in traction. My kids would sneak into the room while I was asleep and add more weights, just to watch me wake up."

Three and a half months later, he was requalified and back to flying.

A CHANCE TO BECOME GENERAL SMITH

Toward the end of his career in the Marine Corps, Colonel Smith was stationed in New Orleans. While there, he became good friends with Congressman Hébert who happened to be the chairman of the armed services committee. "That was big time." He controlled the purchasing for all the armed services. The Congressman and the Colonel enjoyed going out to local restaurants. They could even be found shooting craps with the Maître d', throwing dice up against the ice boxes, having a great time. So, the Colonel bought Hébert a chair, just like his own, but with "The Chairman" on it. They would sit and rock in front of the building on base. They thoroughly enjoyed each other's company.

Escorting Congressman Hébert, the chairman of the Armed Services Committee. He really wanted me to become a General.

Unbeknownst to Haywood, the Congressman thought he would do him a big favor.

He told the Commandant, "If you want to get something done, you need to get the Colonel to come up here to Washington where he can be the liaison between the Marine Corps and Congress. I think you could get a lot more done with Haywood up here."

Well, Haywood did not know anything about it until the general called him and said that they were going to transfer him to Washington. The Colonel made it clear that he was not going to Washington. He had been there for five years, and he did not want to go back. Jeannie, his wife, and he did not want to take the kids back to Washington. He believed they were making the right decision. The Colonel had made a bunch of bad ones, but they thought this was the right one.

The General, though, told him it was going to be a promotion; a one-star billet.

Haywood said that he appreciated it, but he did not think he wanted to do that. They sent him orders, anyway. So, he just put deceased on them and sent them back. Hébert came back down to New Orleans, and he was surprised. He thought that he was going to get the Colonel promoted to general.

Later, the Colonel got a call from the assistant Commandant, and he said, "You can't do that, refusing your orders. You gonna have to come up here. We need you up here in Washington."

So, Congressman Hébert was upset with the Marine Corps and the Colonel missed his chance at being General Smith.

HOW HAYWOOD BECAME THE ONLY MALE MEMBER OF THE RED HAT SOCIETY

Another Haywood Smith was scheduled to speak at the Memphis Peabody Hotel. This Smith was female and president of the Red Hat Society. The Commercial Appeal wrote an article about it but then showed a photo of Haywood Smith, an older male Colonel Haywood Smith.

That stimulated a lot of conversation. His friends called him to say how funny they thought it was. Even a member of the Red Hat Society called to explain what had happened.

> **❝** I will never forget when you and I were confused in the Commercial Appeal. You were a great sport to come on stage and have some fun at our convention in Memphis. **❞**

Haywood Smith, Author, Red Hat Club

When the Red Hat Society meeting occurred, the Colonel showed up for it. When he got to the door, a lady met him and said, "I know who you are!" She recognized him from his photo.

She seated the Colonel in the back where no one would see him. The meeting got underway, and he was the only man in the room. A lady got up and introduced the speaker, "We're so happy to have with us today, Haywood Smith. It's indeed an honor for her to be here with us. Would you please join me in welcoming Haywood Smith?"

The audience applauded and Haywood walked out on stage. He was wearing a red Marine Cap. He received a rousing, standing ovation. It seemed that everyone was apprised of the situation except the other Haywood Smith, who also walked out on stage. Seeing her shock, the Colonel embraced her and they had a little conversation. To everyone's delight, she asked him to stick around for her speech and sit next to her during lunch.

That's how Colonel Haywood Smith became the only male member of the Red Hat Society.

RETIRING FROM THE MARINES

"After retiring at an early age, it's true that I had to readjust. The Marine Corps was very regimented, as was working for the President. Then, all of a sudden, I had no schedule. And it took a while to decide what I might do next."

"I have done some pretty interesting things after retiring. I've worked on secret projects for the government. I've worked for organizations on projects in the desert. I've worked with corporations all over the world. But my family never left Memphis. It was always home. I could have moved, but not Jeannie, so we didn't."

"At one point, several of my friends, dignitaries, CEOs, politicians, and the Memphis State administrators wanted me to come to work for Memphis State as the Assistant Athletic Director. I was resistant but finally agreed to accept the position and see what happened. I enjoyed working with Billy "Spook" Murphy, the Athletic Director. We had some good teams, a strong program, and a wonderful fan base."

Meeting Memphis' Mayor Herenton.

❝ I'm glad you worked with us in the Sports Department at Memphis State. But, the next time you decide to have Tiger Paws painted from the college to the football stadium, would you mind running it past me first? ❞

Spook Murphy Athletic Director, Memphis State

"Sometime during my fairly short career, I thought it would be a great idea to paint Tiger Paws from the campus to the Liberty Bowl. Since a tiger was our mascot, I thought this would be a great idea. I contacted the fellow in charge of roadwork for the city of Memphis and explained my idea to him. He loved it. Then, with the cooperation of several folks in the college, we designed large tiger paw footprints, probably five-feet wide, to be painted like a big tiger's tracks for over two miles on some of Memphis' major roads. As I recall, the city did this at night."

It went over great. The fans loved it. And Haywood was very proud of the Tiger Tracks Team's accomplishment. Something that you can still see on the streets. However, he was soon called into Spook's office. They talked about who was involved and how wonderful the City was in cooperating. Then he asked, "Haywood, did you ever think about getting permission?"

"The smile on my face froze. Permission?"

"You know, like from the president of Memphis State, the Mayor of Memphis, or . . . me?"

That had never crossed his mind. In the Marine Corps, he had learned that as long as the mission was accomplished, he didn't need permission.

"Spook had me pretty worried. Probably because he said he didn't know whether to fire me or salute me. Then he said, 'Fortunately, everybody thinks this was a great idea. And there's not much we can do about it now. We can't exactly take the paws up. So, let me say two things: Good job and please don't do anything like that again.'"

"I thought to myself that this wasn't too different from being in the Marines."

Smith's retirement time has been spent doing a lot of traveling with friends and family. "I've managed to play a lot of golf and have even won several tournaments."

He loves to play poker with friends. He has enjoyed hunting with George Bryan, Fred Smith, Billy Dunavant, and Jeff Smith.

"Lately, I love to fish with Steve in nearby ponds and lakes."

> **I have loved my time with Haywood as we fished and hunted together. We made my son sleep in his room at the hunting lodge. No one else would, due to Haywood's snoring.**
>
> *Jeff Smith, Professional Fisherman*

HAYWOOD AND PRISCILLA

Haywood and Priscilla have belonged to Colonial Country Club in Memphis for many years. Both of their houses backed up to the golf course. "A few years after our spouses died, I received a call from Jim Russell, a good friend of both Haywood's and mine," Priscilla recalled. "He said that Haywood had asked him for my number. Jim asked if it was okay for him to give Haywood my number."

"Of course, I knew who Haywood was. Everyone knew who he was. And from time to time over the years, we visited at social events. I knew he was a gentleman and I thought he was very handsome. Even though Jim was Haywood's friend, he wanted my permission to pass my phone number along. I told him that would be fine."

In a few days, Haywood called and said he'd like to take Priscilla to supper.

"That's how it began." Priscilla, now his wife reflected, "Our relationship blossomed and we have enjoyed many wonderful experiences in life since then. We've traveled all over the world. We've vacationed in wonderful places. Our families have welcomed each of us into their homes and lives. There are so many memories, it makes my head spin."

Haywood sat listening and smiled. "Priscilla has been a true blessing for me and my family. You might find this hard to believe, but I'm not always easy to live with. Priscilla has added so much to my life. Like food in the kitchen and clean clothes!" He let out a hardy laugh. "Beyond that, she has added laughter and thoughtfulness and love."

"Among other things we share is a golf cart," Priscilla said. "We tend to argue over who gets to drive. We also share an evening ritual of working on jigsaw puzzles. I usually pick them out and then we both put them together. We are so proud when we finally finish one!"

Haywood added, "Last night, we sat and stared at the 1,000 pieces scattered across the table, and after two hours, we added six to the puzzle. At this rate, we'll be through in about six months."

A native of Stuttgart, Arkansas, Priscilla thought about her favorite memories with Haywood. "One was visiting the Holy Lands together. That was very

special. A more recent memory was being able to see President Johnson's ranch. We went down there a few months ago with Haywood's family. Haywood showed us where his office was and then took us all around The Ranch. That was a wonderful time."

"I guess neither one of us ever imagined that this is where we would be," Haywood said. "But we are thankful for each other."

HALLOWEEN PARTY

Last year, Haywood and Priscilla decided to go as each other. Priscilla wore Haywood's flight jacket and Haywood surprised everyone with a head full of blonde hair.

Haywood and Priscilla are proving that every day is a gift and meant to lived to the fullest.

> **"** It further reinforced my belief that you and I need to make the most of each day. Wherever we are, whatever our assignment in life is, and whatever our opportunities are. **"**

CHAPTER 6
FROM THOSE WHO KNOW HIM BEST

These thoughts are from Loren Roberts, Professional Golfer and friend:

"I met Haywood through Frank Brown in 1983. Frank was in a golf group with Haywood, George Coors, Ralph Levy, Edgar Bailey, and a couple of others."

"They had a game every Thursday and we'd go to different clubs to play. They became my group of mentors. I was in my late 20s and they were retired. Our friendship continued to grow, and we continued to play together. I think a reason for that was because of our faith in Christ."

"I remember one time we were duck hunting with George Coors in Arkansas. There weren't a lot of ducks around so the next thing I know, Coors wanted to take his plane up to see where the ducks were. I got put in the back seat. George was diving down looking for the ducks and I'd never been so nervous in my life. Finally, Haywood took control and got us safely on the ground."

"If you want to talk about a guy who had a fictitious handicap, it was Haywood. He was so competitive; he'd use it to beat you. He would crank that number to whatever he needed. And he could do it with a straight face. Plus, he was good. He was as good as he needed to be to win the bet."

"His nickname in the golf group was "Kawasaki". He did not hold a golf club in the traditional manner. It looked more like he was pushing the throttle down on a motorcycle handlebar."

"It was really because of my relationship with Haywood and some of the others

"Haywood has always supported and mentored me. He does, however, play by his own set of rules in golf. I cherish our relationship."

Loren Roberts, PGA professional golfer

that I decided to move from California to Memphis. I did not qualify for the Masters that year so I was in Memphis and we were playing golf, when I got the idea to move my family. My daughters were going to start kindergarten the next month and so, the next day, I bought a house. I called my wife and told her that we were moving to Memphis. The contract did allow us to back out, if she hadn't liked it. But fortunately, she loved it. And she liked our group. She had been out to eat with everyone in the group. We moved and I've never been sorry."

"By the way, it was through this group that I met Dr. Cary Middlecoff, winner of two U.S. Opens, One Masters and Three Ryder Cups. We were eating lunch at Memphis Country Club. They were going to play afterwards. Dutch asked Middlecoff if he would come out and give me a golf lesson out on the tee. Middlecoff reluctantly agreed. So, we went out to the teebox. And this is a lesson I now share with all the younger guys who are trying to make it. They are always asking what it takes to become a pro. He gave me one of the greatest lessons I ever received."

"It was about what to do on the tee when you're standing there. We went out on the range. Middlecoff said, 'Okay Loren, I want to see you hit some draws. Hit the ball and make it go right to left.' He knew enough about me to know I was a fader. That was my shot. I hit a few shots and he said, 'Okay, good. I just wanted to know if you could make the ball go right to left because every now and then you're going to have to do that. But when you stand on the tee and you're playing your round, you want to have something on your mind. You need to make the ball curve the same way every time. It does you no good if you aim down the middle of the fairway and you don't know if you're going to hook it or fade it. If you know which direction it's going to curve, you've just simplified your game.'"

"I remember we were playing at Chickasaw one time. My ball would play all four of them. We were at the eighth hole and Haywood and his group made a birdie and thought they had me. I was about 20 yards short of the green with a two so far on a par five."

As Haywood remembered the event, he added, "Roberts was walking around out there, lining it up. I asked Coors what he was doing because he was taking

❝Two things that impress me about Haywood. First, his strong faith in Jesus Christ. Second, his service to our country.❞

Loren Roberts, PGA professional golfer

a long time. To which he replied, 'He's going to try to make the shot for an eagle!'"

Haywood laughed. "And he did! He beat us."

ABOUT GOLF AND HAYWOOD

Roberts further said, "Haywood could handle the pressure. He was always laughing but he could play under pressure. I remember once he was playing in a tournament with George Bryan at Old Waverly in Mississippi. It was the 18th hole, and he had a 15-foot putt. George came up and said to Haywood, 'If you make this we win.' He didn't know that until then. But he made it anyway."

"Two things that impress me about Haywood. First, his strong faith in Jesus Christ. Second, his service to our country. Maybe a third thing is his strength as a father."

"We had a discussion at lunch. Haywood is committed to his faith so much that he was asking what else he needed to do as a Christian. He always feels that he needs to do more. That encourages me. He is always positive. And he is always a good friend who would do anything I needed. He has been so supportive of me, traveling around the country to cheer me on at various PGA tournaments is something I'll always remember."

HAYWOOD AND THE TROUT

Don DeWeese, owner of the iconic Gibson's Donuts in Memphis and longtime friend of the Colonel shared a few memories of his friend:

"Several of us were out there at the beautiful Utah estate of George and Marcia Bryan. George brought a professional fly-fishing guide out to teach us how to fly fish. But if the fish aren't hungry, they aren't going to bite, regardless of how good your teacher is."

"Well, the fish had evidently already been fed that day. I guess that's why we weren't catching anything. I had been there before when we were catching them just as soon as our fly landed on the water."

"Meanwhile, Haywood went to the garage to get a cane pole, came back, put

Don DeWeese and I have played lots of rounds of golf, fished many ponds and traveled the world together.

a piece of bubble gum and some fish food on his hook. Then he threw a cup of fish food out. The fish started churning. He followed up by tossing his bait in the water, right in the middle of the fish food."

"POW! He caught a big, beautiful rainbow trout immediately. The guide didn't know what to think. He'd never seen anybody like Haywood. We all laughed."

"To see my friend, Haywood, figure out a way to catch trout when they weren't biting . . . well that still makes me smile this many years later."

HAYWOOD SMITH GOLF BAG INCIDENT

DeWeese also played golf with Haywood.

"For his age, Haywood is probably the best golfer in the state. He would shoot below his age every time. We were playing number 18 at Old Waverly a couple of weeks before and Haywood was hitting the ball farther than a 65-year-old scratch golfer. Haywood hits the ball over 250 yards on his drive."

"He's that good. But he's also a little on the cheap side. Most golfers start with a new ball. While Haywood does too, he will play a used ball. When he finds one, he puts it in his bag and will eventually use it."

"So, when I find a ball, I put it in my bag. Haywood's back yard backs up to the course. So, whenever we go past his yard, I throw those balls in his pool. I put a green H on each of those balls. Every time I play with him, I see balls with a green H and that's how I know he is using the balls I threw in his pool."

"Well, Haywood had an old golf bag that was faded and looked terrible. Howard Nelson gave me a new golf bag and so I went to the locker storage area and took the clubs and balls out of Haywood's bag and put them into my two-year old bag. I took the old garbage bag and threw it in his pool. When Haywood came out to his pool, he saw the golf bag and assumed the clubs were down there, too. I'm sure he was about to have a fit . . . until he found out what happened. Then he was thrilled."

"One day our round of golf got rained out, so Haywood and I went to his house. I saw all of his memorabilia of the White House, the Marines, Vietnam, Air Force One, the Presidential Flag, photos of Haywood with President Johnson,

> **" Colonel Haywood Smith is one of my most revered friends. Quite simply he amazes me. "**
>
> *Don DeWeese, Owner of Gibson's Donuts*

so many medals and ribbons, letters, photos and autographs from several Presidents, photos of helicopters and fighter jets he flew . . . It's a museum."

HAYWOOD THE DIVER

One of Don's favorite memories of Haywood was during the time Greg Louganis was winning so many diving medals.

"We were at the Men's Grill at the Colonial Country Club one day and we watched him on the TV do a back one and a half with a half twist dive during the Olympics."

Haywood said, "I could do one of those."

Haywood was no spring chicken and that got everybody going, "Haywood, you don't even know where the pool is!"

"So, they started throwing money down. You have to understand that Haywood has his Ph.D. in gambling. But there was no way this old geezer could do the dive we had just seen Greg Louganis do at the Olympics. I saw hundred-dollar bills piled up on the table. Many of the guys were making three, four, and five-hundred-dollar bets. That was a lot of money back then. It still is."

"I knew Haywood, but I didn't know he could dive. So, Haywood gets up and walks out the back way to the Men's Locker Room. It was like the little ducks following the mama duck. Everybody walked down those stairs with him. He walked to his locker and pulled out some swimming trunks."

There wasn't another man in that club that had a swimming suit in his locker. That proved it and DeWeese knew what would happen. Haywood asked the lifeguard if he knew anything about diving. The lifeguard said he was a diver, so it was agreed that he would determine if indeed Haywood had done a back one and a half with a half twist dive.

"Haywood climbed up to the high board and looked over the edge like he was scared. Then he jumped off the board and did a perfect dive. Every one of those men went back into the Clubhouse."

Haywood never did tell any of them that he had been on the Marine Dive Team.

> **“I traveled the country and the world with Haywood. I have no closer friend.”**
>
> *George Bryan, CEO, Sara Lee Corporation, Old Waverly Golf Club*

I WISH WE COULD START OVER

George Bryan, CEO of Sara Lee, President of Bryan Foods and CEO of Old Waverly Golf Course remembers:

"We played in some tournaments together and we won a pretty big one at Old Waverly. He teases me because I told him if he made the final putt we would win."

"I would describe Haywood as a tough Marine who expects others to obey the rules. And he's a good friend, he would do anything for me. He makes me laugh with his quick wit."

"We get along so well because we are both very patriotic. I respect Haywood because he treats everyone the same. If a man doesn't act that way, I don't want to be around him. But, I never played cards with him. I was afraid of him."

"I wish we could start over. That's how good a friend he is."

ANOTHER SKILL

Not everyone realizes just what an impressive poker player Haywood is. Some have accused him of having the ability to memorize cards. Some have accused him of cheating. Some have marveled at his ability to bluff. But they all came around to this conclusion:

Haywood is a great poker player.

Haywood tells the story to Don DeWeese, Gibson's Donuts owner and John St. Clair, NCAA Basketball Referee of over 800 Division I games during lunch one day.

"A man from Arkansas joined Colonial Country Club with a social membership so that he could play in the weekly poker games. In order to play, he needed to be a member of the club. Now this man thought he was a great poker player and could beat all these old men."

"After losing for five weeks in a row, he came back the next week, sat down at the table and started looking at the ceiling. Haywood watched this strange behavior for awhile and asked him what he was looking for."

> **"** I always looked forward to being with Haywood. He was always encouraging and a bright spot. He was also a fierce competitor to this old pro. **"**

Dr. Cary Middlecoff, winner of 39 major golf tournaments including the Masters and the US Open.

The man looked at Haywood and said, "I sure hope y'all have mirrors in the ceiling because I sure hope I'm not this bad of a poker player."

Don and John listened to Haywood's story and smiled. "It wasn't because that fellow was necessarily so bad. It was because he wasn't in the same league from the beginning. He was beaten before he began."

THE NIGHT HAYWOOD WASN'T ROBBED

It was another poker night. Everyone was there. The game was going strong. Most of the players were the same. Some had played together on this night, at this place, for years. They had heard the same stories, laughed at some of the same jokes, and sat in the same seats.

But this night was different.

All of a sudden, two masked men walked into the room. Each was holding an automatic handgun. "Everybody get on the ground and on your stomachs!" one of the bad guys yelled. There was a moment of silence. Then they heard the unmistakable sound of the guns being cocked.

So, everyone complied. They laid on the floor. Everyone except one player. Haywood Smith. The bad guys pointed their guns at him and screamed, "Get on the floor now!"

Haywood looked at them as perhaps only a Marine who has faced death can. He said, "I'm not getting on the floor."

The two masked men looked at each other. This was an unexpected turn of events. They turned their attention to the other poker players, taking their wallets and anything else that was expensive. They turned around and looked at Haywood. He looked at them.

Then they rushed out the door. They were later caught and some of the loot was returned. When asked about his refusal to get down on the floor, Haywood said, "I wasn't going to get down on the floor for them. They could shoot me. Or they could come over and try to get my money. But I wasn't going to get on that floor."

I'M MR. SMITH

Several years ago, the Memphis Fire Department went on strike. It was very controversial. Haywood thought it was not in the best interest of the city. As he drove up to a picket line, he stopped and gave them a "thumbs down" gesture.

As Haywood recalls, a very large man gave his sign to another picketer and walked into the street, straight toward Haywood's car. He actually put his big head inside the driver's side window and said, "Just who do you think you are?"

Haywood placed his 45 pistol against the man's forehead. "Thank you for asking," he said. "I'm Mr. Smith and this is Mr. Wesson."

The man did not anticipate this new development. He recognized too late that he had crossed the line. That's when he fainted.

Haywood held him to keep him from falling and motioned to some of the fellow picketers to come get him. "I didn't like him sticking his head in my window. But I didn't want to leave him in the middle of the street. When his buddies carried him back, they thanked me and apologized for his behavior."

MEMPHIS POLICE DEPARTMENT, STATE YOUR EMERGENCY

Haywood grew tired of all the spam calls and decided to remedy the problem. Whenever the call indicated that it was SPAM, he answered:

Memphis Police Department. Sargent Smith speaking. Please state your emergency.

Click.

Sometimes he took it up a notch.

This is Detective Smith with the Memphis Police Department. We're investigating a murder and are investigating all leads. Because you have called this number, we are going to need to talk to you-"

Click.

“Haywood has been my friend for many years, from back in the 1970s. But there is a competition between us when we step onto the golf course.”

Jim Russell, CEO and owner of Colonial Country Club

INTERVIEW WITH JIM RUSSELL

Jim Russell, CEO and owner of Colonial Country Club and Haywood have been friends for many years, from back in the 1970s. But there is a competition between them when they step onto the golf course.

"I didn't know Haywood during his time in the White House or in Vietnam or in the service in the states. I just knew him as a friend. I did not hear his story from him. Others had told me. And from the start, I admired and had a deep respect for him."

"What I quickly learned was that Haywood had a low tolerance for mistakes in others when he perceived they weren't doing the best they could do. He became that way, I'm sure, from being in the military where he oversaw a large number of Marines and was responsible to many higher-ups himself."

"You have to understand that Haywood expected nothing from others that he didn't expect from himself. He is honest, he has high standards and he is a devout Christian. He is unshakable in his faith. When you understand him, you learn that he is a good man. But we did clash from time to time. We are both strong willed and not afraid to voice our dissatisfaction with another. Therefore, it is accurate to say that we sometimes irritated the other."

Russell and Smith had frequent golf scrambles at the club. He told the golf pro, "Do not pair me with Haywood Smith. We won't make it through a round of golf." So, at the next scramble Jim asked the pro shop who was on his team.

"Haywood Smith."

Jim said, "Whoa. Wait a minute. I specifically asked for him *not* to be on my team."

"Well, I'm sorry Jim. That's who you got."

He quickly found the pro. "I asked you not to pair me with Haywood Smith," he said emphatically. "We're not going to get along well, like I told you, so I'm just going to withdraw."

The pro looked at him with a smile. "Jim, don't worry about it. Haywood has already withdrawn."

> **"Haywood has always been there for me. He was compassionate. He was kind. And he was there."**
>
> *Jim Russell, CEO and owner of Colonial Country Club*

My golfing buddies.

As time went on, a friendship deepened that has overcome any bumps in the road they might have. "He is a great friend that I would do anything for. I can tell him anything in confidence. And he can do the same with me."

One day Haywood asked Jim, "Is there ever anything that you thought you were wrong about?"

Jim just smiled and said, "That's funny, because I was thinking the same thing about you."

Over the years, they've learned how to be good friends and still be candid with each other. "We have developed a need for each other. The need for that close friend you can confide in, but also that close friend you can set straight when you feel like it's appropriate."

One of Haywood's sayings is:
To err is human
To forgive is divine
And neither is my policy.

"Haywood told me, 'You know Jim, when I walk into a room, I used to make somebody really mad in ten minutes. Now it takes me 45 minutes. I must be getting old.'"

"Sometimes we would get so mad at each other on the golf course, I waited for him to get out the cart to make a shot and then left him. He's done the same thing to me."

"Haywood has always been there for me. When I lost my daughter, he was one of the first ones there. He was compassionate. He was kind. And he was there."

Together, they went to West Point, Mississippi for George Bryan's funeral. It was a beautiful service and they truly enjoyed visiting briefly with George's wife, Marcia.

But on the way home, Jim turned a little too soon before Tupelo. They kept driving and driving until Haywood said, "Jim, I think you made the wrong turn back there." Jim agreed, but it was too late to turn around. Normally, to get

to Memphis from West Point, Mississippi, you don't go through Oxford. But they did that day. It took twice as long. Haywood got tickled. He said, "Are you sure you know where you're going now? I don't want to end up in Florida." They laughed all the way back.

Haywood staged a big golf scramble every year at Colonial, called "Pluck a Duck." He would set the golf course up to surprise everyone, like a hole barely larger than the golf ball.

It was truly an event. Haywood was the master of ceremonies. And he served duck to eat. "Have you ever had duck? Not everybody likes it. Including me. But he had the ducks cooked, with dressing and all the sides. Charlie Rogers made the salad. Everybody ate the salad, but hardly anyone wanted Haywood's duck."

"I have many fond memories of my time with Haywood and often think about a Haywood story and just laugh out loud. Joe Williams was an executive at The Commercial Appeal. He lived across the street from me, then moved to Florida. He came back after Jeannie, Haywood's wife, had passed away, and stayed with Haywood."

"You have to remember that Haywood had been in the military, where they waited on him. Jeannie waited on him. She really took good care of him. And Haywood couldn't turn on the dishwasher. So, when Joe got there and it was time to eat, he said, 'Haywood, where's the food?'"

He quickly learned that Haywood didn't go to the grocery store. So, they would eat at the country club every day. Joe was sitting there one morning and the doorbell rang. It was the pest control man who was there to kill bugs. Joe said, You don't have to worry about bugs in this house. "He starved them all to death!"

PLUCK A DUCK

As mentioned by Jim Russell, the "Pluck a Duck" tournament was Haywood's endeavor, in honor of the hunting season. Russell blocked off the day at his Coloniel Country Club for the very popular tournament. The slots filled up quickly. It not only included a wild game meal, but was perhaps the most

unusual golf tournament in the world.

"On some holes, we had the pin sticking up one place but the hole was someplace else. It could be on the other side of the green or maybe just off the green," Haywood explained.

"We moved the tees around so the players sometimes had to hit over the trees."

"One time we put the flag in a sand trap. So the players aimed for the trap. Once they actually got in the trap, they discovered that was not where the hole was. They didn't like that much."

"Another year, we advertised that a special prize would be a car. The closest ball to the hole would win a car. A guy came up and told me that he had indeed won the car."

"With great fanfare, and with everyone at the dinner in tow, I took him outside the club to the driveway and showed him the car he had won. It was a junker that someone had given to me. You couldn't roll down the windows. The paint was peeling. It wouldn't start so it was on a trailer. He was a good sport about it and gave it away."

CINDY AND SUNNY ON MAJOR

Cindy and Sunny, Haywood's daughters, recalled:

"When we lived on the base in Millington, Daddy's driver took us to the bus stop, unless we missed the bus. If we missed the bus, he sometimes took us all the way to school in East Memphis. That's 18 miles. The driver knew where the bus stopped along the way, so he could often catch it at one of its stops."

"Major, our brother, hated school. In New Orleans, when Momma tried to drop him off, he would hold on to the steering wheel and wouldn't let go. By this time the nuns were out there and had to help. Finally, they said they weren't doing that anymore. It was tough with Major. He would get under the bed, and it would take at least two of us to catch him."

"On Saturday, when he didn't have to get up, he got up anyway. Still wearing his pajamas, one Saturday, he took out his little suitcase and packed it with

his stuffed animals, went down the stairs, went out the back door and started walking down the road. When he got to the base gate, the guards would call, 'Colonel, Major is here again.' This was an everyday Saturday activity."

"One of our parents would drive down to the gate and talk to Major. He would tell Dad, 'I'm running away.' Dad would say, 'Okay, son. I'm sorry to hear that because Scooby Doo is on.' Major couldn't get home fast enough."

CINDY AND SUNNY ON HAYWOOD

"Daddy kept the war out of our lives as much as possible. He never talked about it. Ever. However, he would answer questions. He has subsequently shared some of his good experiences with the grandchildren."

"While in Vietnam, Daddy regularly sent us audio tapes. He would tell us how beautiful things were along the ocean. Or how they played volleyball that day. What he ate. He would say, I heard what you were doing. I'm proud of your work. He never told us about the terrible things that were happening."

"Every Sunday afternoon when Daddy was in Vietnam, we'd sit around a tape recorder on the table and talk to him. It was awkward at first, but we got used to it."

FAMILY VACATIONS

"We went to Destin, but sometimes we didn't know it was a vacation. One time we stayed at a nice hotel, and they had a big seafood buffet. We all went. While there, we heard that a waiter had pulled the tablecloth right out from under all the plates, glasses, and silverware. So, Bags, one of Daddy's friends said, "Haywood, watch this!" He stands up, pulls the tablecloth, and everything goes flying. His wife was more mad than embarrassed, but his daughter was mortified, and ran upstairs. Daddy thought it was the funniest thing he'd ever seen."

"One time we were driving from California to Memphis. Daddy knew that we were riding with Momma, but he wanted us to ride with him. He said, 'Girls, you can ride in either car, but mine has air-conditioning.' Of course, we hopped in with Daddy. We looked in the rear-view mirror to see Momma,

198 MY BEST DAY

standing beside her car, getting smaller and smaller."

"After a few minutes, we said, 'Daddy, let's turn on the air-conditioning.'"

"He said, 'Okay, roll down your windows.'"

"When you went with Daddy, you knew there was going to be an event at sometime. We often would go down to Tunica, Mississippi to go fishing. Momma would say, 'Haywood, if the wind is blowing, come home.' Well, sure enough, we'd be way back in the weeds and the wind started blowing and it took a while to get back home."

"The trait that Daddy has is that each of the grandchildren thinks, 'I'm the favorite!' And the last thing that they want to do is to disappoint him. He said one day, 'If I'd known grandkids were so much fun, I'd have had them first.' His love for the grandkids is intense. And they can't do enough to show him how much they love him."

WHILE LIVING IN NEW ORLEANS

"Daddy became the Base Commander in New Orleans. Our house was HUGE! The porch was so big, we had bicycle races on it."

"He liked to invite visitors to our home. He liked to sit on the porch with them, enjoy the view, have a drink and engage in spirited conversation. While Major didn't like going to school, we had a blast. It was a fun place to grow up, and Daddy made it even more fun. You never knew what he might do."

SUNNY AND CINDY ON A VARIETY OF SUBJECTS

The family eventually moved to Millington for Haywood to be the Marine Commander.

On the Millington base, he was held in high regard. So, the girls didn't always tell people who their father was, especially young Marines they might have a crush on.

Sunny remembered it this way, "Daddy decided he needed to be more of a

My kids have always been my pride and joy.

disciplinarian than he was. He would have me sit across the table from him and we would discuss my punishment. He was pretty crafty. If he asked me what my punishment should be, I never knew. If I said, 'I can't go out for the weekend,' he might say, 'Just the weekend?' or he might say, 'Oh, I wasn't thinking that much, but okay.'"

Cindy added, "When Daddy retired, he almost drove my mother insane. He wore a robe until ten. And then would go out and play tennis or golf."

"Daddy is very thoughtful and very generous. The grandkids love him. Everybody has to have their picture with Big Daddy."

"It might be Mother's Day, but everybody wants their photo with *him*," added Sunny, "but not me."

Sunny started thinking of so many things about their father, "Did Daddy tell you he bowled a perfect game? Did he tell you he boxed in the Golden Gloves? He always wins the door prize and people get tired of how much he wins. Lucky? Blessed? He's one of a kind."

INTERVIEW WITH MAJOR

Major, Haywood's son, thought awhile before talking about his dad, "Dad could have been a millionaire several times over, with all his contacts. He had many offers, but he came back to Memphis to live with us."

"My great grandmother called him up and told him his aunt needed help to make the payments on her house. Even with three kids in his house, he paid her house off. That's how Dad operated. He helped his family out with no fanfare."

"Daddy does not judge others. He has said he doesn't know what it's like to walk in their shoes, so he's not going to badmouth them. He does not ostracize them because they made some mistakes. He believes in fair play."

"Dad retired at age 42. That's hard to believe. While all of his friends got up to go to work, he didn't have to do that," Major said. He was offered jobs by Howard Hughes, Armand Hammer, a United States president, a Memphis mayor, and a Marine General. He turned them all down. He wanted to be with us, his family. He said he had been gone long enough."

202 MY BEST DAY

"He never tried to take advantage of his relationships with those folks. Maybe that's why they sought him out. They actually came to see him."

"There's never been another Major in my classes at school or anywhere else for that matter. The reason Dad named me Major is so that I would never outrank him. There is humor in everything he did and does."

THE COKE CAN THAT WASN'T

One night while he was in high school, Major was out drinking with some friends. When he arrived home, he deposited two Coca Cola cans in the fridge and went to bed. About two that morning, his mother came into his room and said, "Maj, your dad is really sick. We don't know why. Everything seemed to be fine when he went to bed. He had just finished a Coke, said goodnight, and went to sleep. Then he woke up, violently ill. Can you think of anything that might have made your father sick?"

Major, still trying to get the cobwebs out of his brain, said he couldn't think of anything. His mother shut the door and he closed his eyes. Suddenly, he sat up, eyes wide open.

"Did she say Coke? I asked myself. I had put two Coke cans in the refrigerator. One was half full of Coke. The other was, well, I used that can to spit tobacco in. I'm not sure why I put it in the refrigerator, but somehow that's what Daddy drank."

"Daddy survived. I don't think he ever knew what was in that can which I quickly threw away."

WAIT . . . THERE'S MORE!

Major thought of one more story, "One time, Mom and Dad left town for a few days. The last thing Mom said was, 'We are trusting you not to throw any wild parties while we are gone.' I assured her that I wouldn't and began calling everybody I could think of to come over for the party."

"And everybody came, too. It was a BIG party. Being underage and having no money, I went to Dad's liquor cabinet. We drank a good bit of his alcohol. At the end of the night, folks were sleeping all over the house. I think I ended up

in a hallway. After most everybody left, I cleaned everything up to the best of my ability. And I had to decide how to deal with the liquor that was missing. I knew Dad would notice the low levels in the bottles. Let's just say that I added nonalcoholic liquids to the alcohol to make it look normal."

"The first problem arose when Mom came into my room on the night they came back. She asked if I knew anything about the cornflakes between the sheets in their bed. I acted shocked and bewildered but I'm quite sure she didn't buy it. The list of suspects was not very long."

"The second problem was the night they invited guests over and poured them some drinks. Needless to say, they didn't taste like rum or bourbon. And needless to say, I was prime suspect."

"I did get in trouble. I think Dad was upset because I violated a trust. He was also probably disappointed that I did something that was so easy to trace back to me."

> **"When Daddy got motivated to take on a house project, he approached it like a military operation. For example, if he needed to change a light bulb, he would say, 'Sunny, go get the ladder. Cindy, find a light bulb. Major, climb that ladder and unscrew the old light bulb.' It worked. Mission accomplished."**

❝ You see, life doesn't end for us just because we retire or because we get a little older. I'm of the opinion that every day should be our best day. Each day is not about our limitations but what we make of that day regardless of any limits we might have. It's the beauty we find in each day. ❞

CHAPTER 7

FROM HAYWOOD

YOUR SPECIAL PURPOSE

"I've heard him say many times that he thinks God has kept him alive this long because He has a 'Special Purpose' for him," Cindy said.

"The only problem," Haywood points out, "is that I haven't found it yet."

"I know Haywood thinks he was spared in Vietnam because God has a 'Special Purpose' for him," George Bryan said. "Maybe the purpose is to encourage people like me. If I got to pick the title of this book, I'd call it Your Special Purpose. Because, when you think about it, the purpose for all of us is to encourage others. If that's the case, Haywood has succeeded. A job well done."

SUNSETS AND FIRST STARS

"Every evening, I look out over the golf course, just on the other side of my backyard. I love to see the sunset. Then I wait for the first star. Depending on the time of year, it comes out anywhere from 7:00 to 8:00. When it comes out, I always say a little poem."

"Starlight, starbright, First star I see tonight,
I wish I may, I wish I might,
Make this wish, I wish tonight."

"Then I make a wish. Then I come in."

"I try to get out there every night. I take a drink with me. I use the time to think about the day and to think about my friends. My wishes are often for my friends."

"You see, life doesn't end for us just because we retire or because we get a little older. I'm of the opinion that every day should be our best day. Each day is not about our limitations but what we make of that day regardless of any limits we might have. It's the beauty we find in each day."

"In the last ten years, I have made a conscious effort to enjoy each day. To understand that there will be problems and setbacks, even heartaches, but also to understand that each day is a precious gift that I shouldn't take for granted."

"One of the things I do is to keep up with my friends. I do that through meals, phone calls, and letters. There's one group of some of my Marine Corp buddies that meets some place every year. I have another Marine Corp friend that I talk to once a week. Every Tuesday morning."

"I try to get together once a week with a group of friends in the Memphis area. We call it the Liars Lunch. It's usually about ten of us. We pick a restaurant and spend an hour or two catching up. That's a lot of fun."

"Several of my friends stop by to see me a couple of times a month. I play golf with some other friends three or four times a week. I also play cards with some friends twice a week. Priscilla and I try to eat out with friends a few times a month."

"I go on a trip a few times a year with friends. We usually play golf some. I've also been on fishing trips and hunting trips with them."

"It all goes back to me knowing that life won't last forever and I don't want to miss out on being with and helping those I hold most dear."

MY PRAYER LIST

"For many years, I've used a prayer list. It's about three full pages of folks I pray for *each day*. I take the prayer list very seriously. And I welcome taking them off the list. I want to pray for you when you are sick or going through a tough time. After that, I mark you off. I know that sounds hard, but if I didn't

> "You must enjoy what you do in life. If you don't, you've made a mistake."

I went to a Halloween party as Priscilla.

mark people off, I'd have 20 pages which would take hours."

"This was a shock to Steve Williford, who has been helping me write this book. He had been sick for a couple of days, and I had told him that he was on my prayer list. One day over the phone, I asked how he was doing, and he said he was much better. I said to wait for a minute. When I came back on the phone, Steve asked what I did."

"I just marked you off my prayer list."

"He didn't like that too much, but I can't help it. He got better."

DO WHAT YOU LOVE

"If you've made it this far reading this book, I want to thank you for letting me share my life with you. I've never thought of it as unusual, but I'm frequently told it has been. Maybe so. I do know that I've enjoyed it. Which brings me to a final thought before I say goodbye."

"Over the years, many men and women, military and civilian, young and old, have asked for my advice for what they should do next in their lives. Let me share with you what I tell them. Maybe you need to hear this, too."

"You must enjoy what you do in life. If you don't, you've made a mistake. And sometimes, due to circumstances, you have to find joy in what you do."

"Whatever you do, be the best. Take pride in your work. I don't care what it is, if you can't wait until you get to work, you'll be a success. You have to have desire inside yourself. A lot of people go to college for something they really don't want to do."

"I was proud to put on the uniform every day. I was proud to be seen in it. I wore it with dignity and respect. That's true for everyone. Look forward to what you do every day."

"And it's okay to laugh and have fun at work. Even on the battlefield, I searched for humor. It kept us going. Find something you can laugh about even if you're in the hospital or very sick or stressed out."

"Find the joy in your job.

Find the joy in your family.

Find the joy in cooking out.

Find the joy in sharing
a meal with a friend.

Find the joy in helping a friend.

Find the joy in each day.

And then find the joy
in tomorrow."

214 MY BEST DAY

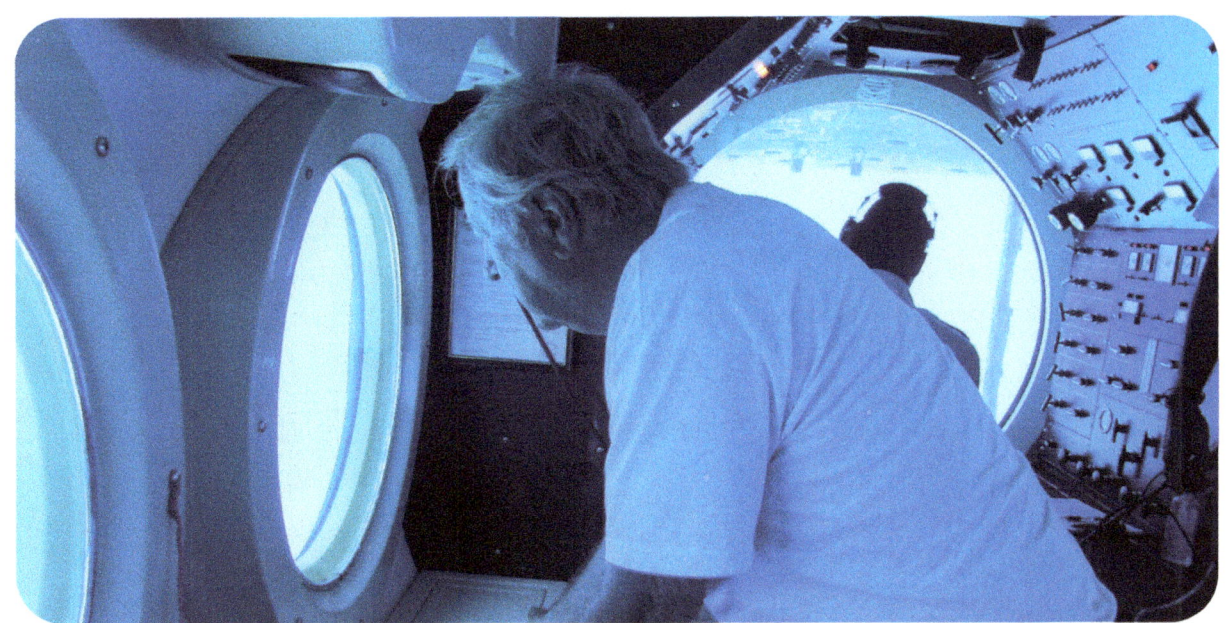

MY BEST DAY 215

EPILOGUE

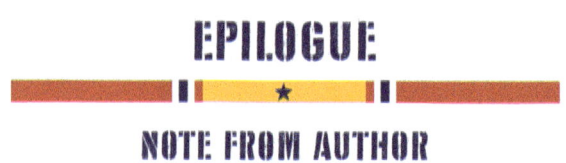

NOTE FROM AUTHOR

Life goes on for Colonel Haywood Smith. Every day is filled with joy. Or maybe that's my perspective. That is, my life has more joy because of him. We talk almost every day. He's become not just another writing client, but also a dear friend. And do you know why? Because I'm his dear friend.

Here's what I've learned. That's the way Haywood operates. If he's your friend, he's a part of your life. And you are a part of his. He asks me questions about what's going on in my life, my trips, my house, my pets, my children, and my day. For example, he called me last night about 9:00.

Colonel: Hey Bud

Steve: Hey Colonel

Colonel: I was just calling to see how you're doing. You know, when I don't hear from you for a couple of days, I have to check to make sure you're doing okay. Are you doing okay? Are you sick? Are you in the hospital? Do you need bail money?

Steve: All is well. I've been out of town.

Colonel: Good. I was hoping I didn't have to come bail you out. That could get expensive.

Here's another conversation.

Steve: Hey Colonel, what are you doing?

Colonel: Oh, I'm just sitting here working on a puzzle Priscilla got me for Christmas.

Steve: How's it coming?

Colonel: Well, I've been at it for about an hour and I've found one piece.

Steve: How many pieces in the puzzle?

Colonel: One thousand. At this rate, I calculate I'll be through in eight years.

On the occasion of Haywood's 92nd birthday, I wanted to give him something that would mean something but at the same time be useful.

Then it hit me. I had the perfect gift for him. I knew one of his golfing buddies, and a person he truly respected, was Bud Davis, the owner of Bud Davis Cadillac in Memphis.

One year I gave Bud a beautiful pen and letter opener set for his birthday. The handles were handmade out of Olive Tree wood from the Holy Lands. Bud said that meant a lot to him and thanked me profusely.

Bud passed away a couple of years later. I asked Gary, his son, if he minded if I got a momento from Bud's office. He took me into Bud's office and looked around with me. He opened Bud's desk drawer and there was the pen set in its beautiful wooden box. Bud had never used it. So I asked Gary if I could have that.

I gave Haywood that set. I told him that I knew he had visited the Holy Lands and would appreciate the wood. I knew that he received a lot of mail and needed a letter opener. And I knew how much he thought of Bud. Then I told him the story.

Haywood thanked me for the gift and said he would definitely use it every day. I could tell his brain was working. When I left that day, he thanked me again and said, "By the way, don't think about trying to get this back again when I pass away."

Stephen Williford

INDEX

Adenauer, Konrad ... 59
Anders, William ... 92
Astrodome First Baseball Game ... 88-89, 91
Bailey, Edgar ... 173
Borman, Frank ... 92
Brenner, Bags ... 15
Brown, Russell ... 73, 75
Brown, Frank ... 173
Bryan, George ... 169, 177, 182-183, 191, 193, 207
Bryan, Marcia ... 177, 191
Clifton, Ted ... 43, 76-77, 81
Cole, Cindy Smith ... 3, 194-202, 204, 205, 207
Conger, Colonel ... 37, 39
Connally, John ... 59, 88, 90-91, 93
Coors, George "Dutch" ... 173, 175
Cross, Jim ... 43, 60, 87, 89
Cuban Missile Crisis, The ... 34, 37
Darracott, John ... 131
de Gaulle, Charles ... 98, 99, 101
DeWeese, Don ... 2, 177-181, 183, 185
Dunavant, Billy ... 167
Eisenhower, Dwight D. ... 93, 116
Ellington, Buford ... 80-81
Football, The ... 9, 81, 83, 85
Freckles ... 64-65, 67
Gandhi, Mahatma ... 64
Glenn, John ... 92
Graham, Billy ... 59, 68, 85
Halaby, Najeeb ... 61, 63
Herenton, Willie ... 166
Haywood's Hooch ... 114-117, 129, 131, 135, 137, 145
Hébert, Edward ... 160-163
Hoover, Herbert ... 93
Hoover, J. Edgar ... 86-87, 93
Hope, Bob ... 30-31, 33
Hughes, Howard ... 73, 203
Hussein, bin Talal ... 44
Jennings, Jack ... 31, 33, 152, 153, 155
Joan of Ark ... 157
Johns, Lem ... 99
Johnson, Lyndon B. ... 9, 40-47, 50-59, 62-69, 71-75, 77, 79-97, 99-107, 131, 171, 179
Johnson, Luci Baines ... 45, 47-49, 64, 65
Johnson, Lady Bird ... 45, 51, 59, 67, 73, 75, 85, 87, 88, 93, 96, 97, 103

Johnson, Sam 69, 71
Kennedy, John F. 43, 51, 59, 61, 93, 100, 151
Kissinger, Henry 109
LBJ Ranch, The 41, 43, 45, 50-51, 58-61, 63, 67, 69, 73-79, 89-91, 97-107, 131, 171
Lee, Dr. Robert Greene 17
Leigh, Janet 9, 94-95
Levy, Ralph 173
Lovell, Earl 35, 155, 157
Lovell, Jim 92, 155
Luminous Six 138
MAG-16 .... 109-111, 131-132, 139
Marble Mountain 7, 9, 110-115, 120-123, 137, 143-147
McCarver, Tim 27
McGovern, George 59
McNamara, Robert 41, 151
Meeks, Dale 61
Middlecoff, Cary 175, 184
Murphy, Billy "Spook" 165-167
Musial, Stan 9, 103, 156
Neubauer, Sally Snyder 52-53, 55, 57
Nitze, Paul 41
Nixon, Richard 47, 59, 107-109
Nurses Visit Marble Mountain 147, 149
Okamoto, Yoichi 58, 63, 65, 69
Onasis, Jacqueline Kennedy 100
Percy Preist Dam Dedication 79-81, 83
Perot, Ross 149-151
Presidential Flag, The 104-105, 179, 181
Red Hat Society, The 163-165
Robb, Lynda Bird Johnson 45-48
Roberts, Loren 173-177
Roosevelt, Franklin 93
Rusk, Dean 93
Russell, Jim 169, 188-193, 195
Sequoia, The 93, 95
Smith, Fred 7, 112-113, 115, 167
Smith, Jeannie 3, 28-32, 35, 71, 163, 167, 195
Smith, Jeff 167-168
Smith, Major 3, 194-207
Smith, Priscilla Robinson 3, 169-171, 210-211, 216
Tattoo Lady, The 19
The Python, Alice 125
Truman, Harry 59, 62-63, 93
University of Memphis, The 25, 27
USS Enterprise, The 34, 37

220 MY BEST DAY

Vance, Cyrus 101
von Braun, Werner 9, 95
Warren, Chief Justice Earl 72-73
Watermelon Heist, The 21, 23
Williams, Joe 193
Williamson, Sunny Smith 3, 194-202, 204-205
Williford, Steve 2, 9, 167, 211, 215, 216
Youngblood, Rufus 79, 81, 99